"We have taken our stand on the side of Korea and our pledge of faith to that nation is a witness to all the world that we champion liberty…"

-Harry S. Truman
President of the United States
June 27, 1950

"It's not really the chicken, or the broth, although they have nutrients, and all that. It's you, the maker, the cook. You put your *self* in Chicken Soup, you know? Pray in it, if you like. That's what tenderizes the moment."

-Gloria S. (Mrs. James R.) Baker
Mother of Glory Sugar Baker
September, 1968

"God is Love – and versa visa"
Esco (Richard Farnsworth)
"Resurrection"

Honey Baby Darlin'
Book One — The Farm

is dedicated to the 60th Anniversary of the Korean War, to
Peace, to families everywhere who face separation and worse
by war, and to the hope for a future built on love.

Book One — The Farm
is also dedicated to my biological-cousin and heart-sister,
Babe Conroy, who said to me,
"Drop everything and write this book."

Author's Note

There I was, creating a memoir in four enormous chapters about 60 eventful years of cooking, when my mind got fortuitously snowed in with La Muse at a gentleman's farm in Ohio during the harsh winter of 1951-52, and stayed for a blooming summer. My alert Muse and I built an imaginary fire, settling in for a long look at my bedrock of kitchen craft: the Farm's big, warm country kitchen, a scene of continual culinary activity, a pantry full of surprises, a cup of romance, a scant teaspoon of the dark, and a woman made lonely but inspired to nurture by war.

The Farm kitchen recipe binders are true cooking histories, written by hand, with pages stained with the chocolate fingerprints of real people, who, with a whiffle!, came shimmering to life in my kitchen, sticking spoons into sauces, whispering "less flour" or "more stock." With these folks came their identities, and not just a few of their ideas. Woven into the fabric of this memoir are nuggets from the forgotten letters of two lovers separated by an ocean of longing.

Nurturing people with beautiful delicious food - honoring the kitchen as a temple and the home as a studio of nourishment - all this that fills my heart - came first from the Farm. Simmer it down to Love.

Chapter One became **Book One**.

Honey Baby Darlin' is a serial memoir about cooking, love, and the love of cooking. We'll just start at the beginning: **Book One —The Farm**.

Time enough for growing up; cooking for big famous people; antics of infamy; bakeries and cafes.

All characters are renderings. All recipes and historical nuggets are as true as possible.

Ginna BB Gordon

Introduction

"HoneyBaby?"

"Yes Ma'am?"

"What you want in your lunch pail t'day, Darlin'?"

Flossie knew I had a thing for food.

Thus begins the first part of my culinary adventures.

My name is Glory Sugar Baker.

Honey Baby Darlin',

Book One - The Farm is the name of this story.

In the summer of 1951, before my father, James R. Baker, Warrant Officer and Bandleader, went off to the Korean War with the Army, he shepherded his little flock from San Francisco, in a 1950 Ford Woodie Station Wagon, across the wide country: my mother, Gloria, my brother, Martin, 6, and me, Glory, 4. We left a Sunset District bungalow Gloria named the Little Jewel Box, in the warm, friendly climate of the west coast, and prepared for an Ohio winter on my grandfather's farm.

In the fire-warmed kitchen of the Sugar Farm, Flossie & Bessie gave their all to the general sustenance of the Farm Folk and the keeping of the Big House. Lincoln managed the garden and the Coop. Backstairs, above the kitchen-wing, their rooms were at the top of wide glossy-white steps, which climbed around the west end of the Big House. At the east, in the foyer, rose a curving staircase with mahogany banister, excessively carved and polished to a dark gleam, down which I actually did slide once. Carpeted in rich, thickly padded maroon wool, patterned with black and green dragons, these stairs led to the plushy forest green rooms of my grandparents, John Elliott and Maria Monique (Pop and Marnie) Sugar; Sucre, if you go back far enough in the lineage. On the tall, canopied bed with tufted green velvet headboard, so high the stool barely gave me purchase onto the mattress, I curled up under fluffy green eiderdown quilts. Between the Folks' bedrooms in the east wing and Backstairs in the west was a long dark, narrow hallway, with black and white checkered linoleum, sleek with wax - good for "sock-skating."

Upon her arrival home at the Farm, Gloria bustled her way into the Big House kitchen. Cooking became her passion, to pass the time. Flossie and Bessie bore her no ill will. Flossie said to me, "HoneyBaby, she fills dat hole of her loneliness with dis lovely dough." They were glad to see her back.

She was beautiful, our Gloria. 5 foot two, eyes of blue - in college she was "Be," "BE," "Bedroom Eyes." Her lips were high-gloss Truly Red; hair in short, fluffy blonde curls; her beauty: elfin, compact. The story goes that Gloria unknowingly seduced James with her mellifluous voice during a radio serial performance — after he heard it, he went to the studio to find out just who *was* this woman who had so captivated him; he couldn't get her voice out of his mind.

He was on leave from the Army during World War II. "I remember it was pouring rain," he told us at least annually for the duration of their forty-some year marriage. "I put on my hat and raincoat and galoshes and hopped the bus to WCLE. They stopped me at the door, but smiled at my uniform and let me pass when I told them I was in love with this mysterious-voiced woman I was about to meet, and that I had come to escort her home under the umbrella I brought along for that very special privilege."

I believe she was his from hello.

James' letters sustained Gloria during that first year at the Farm, though the sweetness of his words made her lonelier, surrounded as she was by small children with winter illnesses, her parents, siblings, staff, animals and mounds of mid-winter snow. James wrote of little things and big — in San Francisco, as he readied himself for a 15 day ocean crossing on a cargo ship bound for Japan, he shared with her his shopping list ("round toothpicks, miniature clothespins, clothesline, paper cups, lighter fluid and flints, bunch of assorted nails, Alka Seltzer, sewing kit — forgot a flashlight — forgot pictures of my family").

James

San Francisco

Aug 31st 1951

A novel gadget!

A typewriter which rents for 30 cents a minute!

It sits on a table in the Officers' Club

Solves my handwriting challenges for a while

Boat sails next Wednesday.

Miss you and your warm behind in bed

Can't dwell on it — don't want to cry in public

Trying not to let my thoughts linger on how much I miss you

James kept a journal of his crossing for Gloria — poems written in his own loneliness and desolate boredom; detailed descriptions of his fellow officer shipmates; complete menus of the food ("had a choice of eggs or flapjacks — was ravenously hungry — made myself look completely pitiful and asked for both! — limp bacon, toast, *margarine*, ugh!, pots of suspiciously-red strawberry jam, not like yours"). He penned poems and tapped out love songs on his knee ("I like what I see when I look in your eyes, my Gloria… the love that is there like the sun lights the skies, my Gloria…").

The journal and letters lived in a closet for 25 years after the deaths of James and Gloria, in a shoebox held together by wide swaths of black electrical tape. They kept me company in a vague, indistinct, invisible way: I never had the courage, or the willingness, to invade their privacy to read them.

One morning, while struggling over a paragraph about Gloria's general gloomy mood in 1951 at the Farm, La Muse floated into the room, clutched my sleeve in long, slender, transparent fingers and danced me down the hall to the closet. "Wake up woman!" she fluttered in my ear. "You don't have to make this up!"

In a Muse-led trance, I reached up to the top shelf and pulled down a shoebox, suddenly realizing that what I had in my hands was the key to my parents' love, the treasure box of my family

The inheritance. I surrendered and read.

James
The Journal
Onboard ship —
Sept 8th, 1951

The sea rolls
Saw the movie Harvey
with the troops
for the third time
36 men in a sleeping compartment!
So close — the air is thick with man-scent
Everyone is sea sick — mal de mer
Wish I'd gotten aboard regular transport
My Gloria, hope that all this is not useless

James
The Journal
Onboard ship —
Sept 9th1951

The sky is azure — the sun is out —
The ocean deep, deep cobalt
And still rolling, rolling, rolling
Sick sick sick
I look like a tramp
Haven't bathed since last Sunday
Haven't shaved since Tuesday
Haven't felt much like writing at all
Much less sharing my often wild ideas
The sunset last night was so beautiful
And I *saw* you in it
But not for long,
Tears cloud my vision

Several days after gifting me with this treasure, whoosh! in Madame La Muse came again, reading over my shoulder the bit I was writing about Gloria's special Red Binder cookbooks. La Muse tapped me on the noggin with her goose quill pen. I *have* those books, I thought, in a sudden rush of brilliance, and went to the cupboard.

Back there, in 1951, I followed Gloria into the Big House kitchen and sat at the feet of goddesses of farm cuisine, collecting memories *of* and filling myself *with* the love Gloria poured into her food and family while trying not to be maudlin about her lover's absence. I took note of dark rich poultry stocks and flaky pastry; absorbed Flossie's burbling commentary about canning beans in hot jars and pickling cucumbers in big sticky barrels full of brine. Gloria's butter came from the cream top of fresh milk brought home from Harmon Cobb in big tin pails. Martin and I and our cousins, Little Jon and T, Jr., cultivated harmony among Lincoln's coop of Rhode Island Reds, so better to reach under their warm little feathered behinds for eggs to give substance to our custards and pies. The aroma of bread baked with molasses was the perfume I wished to dab behind my ears.

Honey Baby Darlin', Book One - The Farm tracks the first leg of the journey of a girl cook, on a quest to create beauty, to nurture, to comfort and to please palates: to hear the sighs of the well-fed. Tools, pantry, recipes, and some culinary observations are herein. This book is for people who love food, cooking, beauty, a little history and wartime romance. It is carefully tended for the details of creation and filled with the love of kitchen-craft. All recipes serve six to eight, unless otherwise noted.

Four voices tell this story: James, Gloria, Little Glory and her grown up self,

Glory Sugar Baker 2011

The Farm

HoneyBaby?"

"Yes Ma'am?"

"What you want in your lunch pail t'day, Darlin'?"

"Ha! **French Bread** with **Smoked Salmon Salad**! My favorite!"

"I thought Tuna was your favorite," she said.

"Yes, but that was yesterday, before I had smoked salmon!"

The morning dialogues with Flossie were like this.

When we moved to the Farm, Gloria's replacement passion was cooking, pretty much anything - she was compelled to nurture. The Farm Guest Cottage, where we lived during our years at the Sugar Farm, seemed too small for her without James in it — her restless spirit pushed Gloria up the path to the Big House, humming his knee-tapped tunes:

"The one hope for me is that I'll always see, my Gloria."

She woke before dawn, put on a checked or dotted or brightly colored shirtwaist dress, seamed stockings and heels (yes, yes, seamed stockings and heels, she really did), leaned over the back Dutch door of the cottage smoking a cigarette in a carved ivory holder while her coffee perked. Shrugging on a coat, she clattered up to the Big House, steaming cup in hand. She was in the kitchen at 5am, already dusted with flour from apron to nose, hands wrapped around a big mound of smooth, elastic dough.

"I'm lucky, I know, I can claim you for mine, my Gloria."

When Martin awoke, bundled himself and then me in the big thick oversized jackets, our "outdoor robes," guided me up the little path, sleepy-eyed, groggy-faced, ready for breakfast, the fire was lit and the broad hearth was covered with dough rising in cloth-topped bowls. As I came in the door, I smelled **Wheat Bread** sweetened with molasses and studded with raisins, fragrant with cinnamon. Maybe cardamom — yes! **Hot Cross Buns**!

"I promise to love you as long as stars shine, my Gloria."

James
Sept. 7th, 1951
Onboard ship —
The Journal Bookmark
[a torn strip off a page
-scribbled at 45 degrees]

Note!
Assignment not certain
Don't mail letters yet
Read this book at leisure
Love you
ME

The Big House Kitchen

The Big House kitchen was divided in two by a polished oak plank counter with six oak, backless stools. On one side, the cooking area: six burner stove, two ovens, double sinks facing the back acres, pantry. On the other side: six foot oak plank table set into a corner, with a built-in bench along the wall under paned windows overlooking Lincoln's garden. The wide stone fireplace gracefully filled the opposite wall. On the other side of the black swinging door, the formal dining room sat dark and forlornly empty when my grandparents were not in residence. The rest of us flocked to the kitchen: Gloria, Martin and me; my cousins Little Jon and T (Tournier) Jr., who always seemed to be at the Farm, though they lived in town; the "colored folks" - Flossie, Bessie, Lincoln, Mr. Talbot; and Mark Johnson, Martin's buckeroo, who lived in the Bunkhouse, tending and mending the rest of the Farm. He wore cool boots and sometimes chaps over his jeans when he was working with a horse. Martin called him "Slick."

French Bread

2 tablespoons active dry yeast
2 tablespoons sugar
4 cups lukewarm water
8 cups sifted white flour
1 teaspoon salt

In a large bowl, dissolve the yeast and sugar in lukewarm water. Let stand for two minutes. Stir in half the flour and the salt. Add just enough of the remaining flour to hold the dough together — it will form soft, slightly sticky dough.

Knead in the bowl for about five minutes, adding just enough more flour to assist kneading and not stick to your hands. Cover and let rise until double, 1-2 hours. Set near a warm oven or fire to quicken the rising process.

Preheat the oven to 400°.

When the dough has risen, punch it down with your hand and divide into loaves: two medium loaf pans, two baguette pans or one large loaf pan. Clay will produce a great crust. Let rise again for 1/2 hour to 45 minutes, or until the dough has risen over the top of the pan(s).

Bake for about forty minutes on the middle rack. Place trays of water on the rack below. The loaves will be brown and crusty when they are done. Pierce with skewer for doneness — if they come out clean, that's that! Cool one hour before slicing.

Smoked Salmon Salad with Cornichons

1 8 oz. package smoked salmon

1/2 cup cornichons, chopped

2 green onions, minced

2 chopped hardboiled eggs

Salt to taste

Pepper to taste

1/2 teaspoon dill

1/2 teaspoon honey mustard

2 tablespoons mayonnaise

Mix well. Refrigerate.

Cornichons (gherkins)

6 pounds (about 40) tiny fresh picked cucumbers, 1-2 inches long each

1 1/2 cups coarse (kosher) salt OR 1 1/4 cups pickling salt

1/4 cup white wine vinegar or distilled white vinegar

18 sprigs fresh tarragon

6 shallots, peeled and sliced thin

1 tablespoon mustard seed

1 tablespoon black peppercorns

2 quarts white wine vinegar, more if needed

Wash cucumbers in cold water and remove any blossoms. Rinse and drain. Mix with salt in stainless steel or ceramic bowl. Cover the bowl with a cloth and let stand at room temperature for 24 hours. Stir to keep the brine which forms well mixed. Next day, drain the cucumbers and rinse in 3 quarts of cold water and 1/4 cup white wine vinegar or distilled white vinegar. Let stand 15 minutes. And let dry.

Scald and drain a 1 gallon crock. Approximate your layers and divide ingredients into that number. Layer: Tarragon, cucumbers, spices. Repeat until crock is filled about 2/3 of the way. Pour in enough white wine or distilled vinegar to cover the cucumbers and seasonings by 2 inches. Cover the crock with a plate on which you set a brick or heavy weight. Leave the pickles in a cool, dark spot for a month, after which they will be ready to use.

Tuna with Pickles

1 can albacore tuna, drained and flaked
1/2 cup bread and butter pickles, chopped and drained
2 green onions, minced
2 chopped hardboiled eggs
1 small can chopped black olives
Salt to taste
Pepper to taste
Pinch tarragon
1/2 teaspoon honey mustard
2 tablespoons mayonnaise
Mix well. Refrigerate.

I watched Harmon's sister, Doris, place a 40 gallon barrel in the barn in a dark corner, and prepare cucumbers and a briny solution in her kitchen in big buckets that she hauled to the barn on a little flatbed cart. She filled the barrel from the buckets, placed a flat wooden lid on top and left it. Every time someone wanted a pickle, they just went to the barn!

Bread and Butter Pickles
Makes about ten 12 oz. jars of pickles

15 cups sliced pickling cucumbers
3 onions, thinly sliced
1/4 cup coarse salt
4 cups crushed ice
2 1/2 cups apple cider vinegar
2 cups sugar
3/4 teaspoon turmeric
1/2 teaspoon celery seed
1 Tablespoon brown mustard seeds

Combine cucumbers, onions, salt and ice in a large bowl. Mix well. Put a weight on it (a plate with a brick on it works well) and allow to stand 5 hours. Drain thoroughly.

Combine vinegar, sugar, turmeric, celery seed and brown mustard seed in a large pot. Add drained cucumbers. Place pot on medium low heat.

Bring almost to a boil, but DO NOT ALLOW TO BOIL.

Remove from heat. Seal in sterilized jars, 10 minutes in a hot water bath.

To sterilize jars: Wash them well in hot soapy water and dry them off.

Place on a cookie sheet, right side up, at 225°F for 15 minutes. Turn off oven and leave them in there until you need them.

If you increase the spices and add some grated ginger, these are quite sparkly with Indian food.

James
Sept 8th, 1951
Onboard ship —
Journal Foreword

My Gloria,
This little book…
Is a substitute for letter writing…
One long, shipboard missive to my wife
Whom I love so deeply
(And whose **Count Pavel's Beef Stroganoff**
I long for in my dream)
Continuous thoughts
Miscellaneous stories,
A playground for words
It requires only one mailing and
I shall write as the spirit moves me
Hopefully daily

In the Kitchen with Gloria

*Gloria's background music while making **Count Pavel's Beef Stroganoff**: Tchaikovsky 's "Swan Lake." When James was around, he played Chopin on the piano for her while she cooked, to keep her dancing in the kitchen, he said. While he was away, she kept the portable record player on the table, in order to hear something akin to his music she sorely missed — she played James' collection of 33 1/3 LPs, "platters" of symphonies, piano solos and show tunes. Gloria would often be found stone still in the middle of some kitchen activity, staring at the window, as if she were watching a movie in the thick glass, "Swan Lake" or "Peer Gynt" or maybe Bing Crosby her soundtrack.*

Count Pavel's Beef Stroganoff

The real Count Pavel Stroganoff was a dignitary of some sort at the court of Alexander III, a member of the Imperial Academy of Arts, and a well-known gourmet, who lost all his teeth, for which Beef Stroganoff was invented for his toothless delight! So the story goes.

Makes 4 servings

1/2-pound piece well-trimmed beef tenderloin,
cut into 2x1x1/2 inch strips
2 tablespoons vegetable oil
Flour for dredging
6 tablespoons (3/4 stick) butter
1/4 cup finely chopped shallots
1 pound mushrooms, sliced
1 cup beef stock
2 tablespoons sherry
3/4 cup sour cream
1 tablespoon Dijon mustard

12 ounces wide egg noodles or rice
1 tablespoon paprika

Be sure meat is dry, patted between two paper towels. Sprinkle with salt and pepper and dredge in flour. Heat the oil in heavy large pan. Working in batches, add meat in single layer and cook just until brown on outside, about 1 minute per side. Transfer to parchment lined baking sheet.

Melt 2 tablespoons butter in same skillet over medium-high heat. Add chopped shallots and sauté until tender, scraping up browned bits, about 2 minutes. Add mushrooms. Sauté until liquid evaporates, about 10 minutes. Add beef stock, then Cognac. Simmer until liquid thickens, about 14 minutes. Stir in cream and Dijon mustard. Add meat and any accumulated juices from baking sheet. Simmer over medium-low heat about

2 minutes, until meat is heated through but still medium-rare. Season to taste with salt and pepper.

Meanwhile, cook the noodles in large pot of boiling salted water until tender *per package instructions. Drain. Transfer to bowl. Add remaining 4 tablespoons butter and toss to coat. Season with salt and pepper. Divide noodles among plates. Top with beef and sauce. Sprinkle generously with paprika.

*If you prefer rice, cook per instructions. Although not traditional, chopped fresh or dried parsley is lovely sprinkled on top, in addition to the paprika.

For Chicken Stroganoff:

1 boneless chicken breast, pounded thin and cut in small pieces.

Toss chicken pieces in flour and proceed above as with beef, with two exceptions: after browning the small bits of chicken, remove from pan with slotted spoon. Cook the rest of ingredients, using chicken stock instead of beef, and place the crispy chicken on top of the sauce when serving.

James
The Journal
Onboard ship —
Monday, Sept. 10ᵗʰ, 1951

And my son is seven years old today
I can't send a cable because
The ship is maintaining
radio silence
But I am with him in my heart
I ask myself,
Have I done a good job?
Is he a good boy?
He's a wonderful boy!
Can I take any credit?
It's all you, Gloria
My Gloria
There are haunting themes
Bothering me today
Songs roll around in my head
"Stella by Starlight"
"Laura"
"Too Young"

Quick Wheat Bread with Raisins

God Bless our Gloria for this little motherly specialty: French Bread with part whole wheat flour and molasses to make it more robust. She thinly sliced it for banana and peanut butter sandwiches, toasted it for breakfast, but, best of all,

floated it in warm milk (Milk Toast) for four cousins getting over the flu.

2 tablespoons active dry yeast
1/4 cup black strap molasses (the darker, the better)
4 cups lukewarm water

4 cups sifted white flour
4 cups sifted whole wheat flour
1 teaspoon cinnamon
1-2 cups raisins
1 teaspoon salt

In a large bowl, dissolve the yeast and molasses in water. Let stand for two minutes. Stir in half the flour, the raisins and cinnamon and the salt. Add just enough of the remaining flour to hold the dough together — it will form a soft, slightly sticky dough.

Knead in the bowl for about five minutes, adding just enough flour to assist kneading so the dough won't stick to your hands.

Cover and let rise until double, 1-2 hours. Set near a warm oven or fire to quicken the rising process.

Preheat the oven to 400°.

When the dough has risen, punch it down with your hand and divide into loaves: two medium or one large loaf pan. Clay will produce a great crust. Let rise again for 1/2 hour to 45 minutes, or until the dough has risen over the top of the pan(s).

Bake for about forty minutes on the middle rack. Pierce through with skewer to test doneness. If skewer comes out clean, you're done!

Hot Cross Buns

1 cup scalded milk
1/2 cup butter, room temp.
1/2 cup sugar
1 teaspoon salt
1 cake compressed yeast
1 egg, well beaten

About 4 cups sifted white or wheat
(or combination) flour
3/4 teaspoon cinnamon
1/4 teaspoon cardamom
1 cup currants

1 egg

1 tablespoon water

Pour the scalded milk over the butter, sugar and salt; cool to lukewarm. Add the crumbled yeast and let rest for 5 minutes. Add the egg, cinnamon and cardamom and enough flour to make a soft dough. Fold in the currants. Let rise in a warm place (80 to 85°) until double - about 2 hours. Cut into about 24 equal pieces and shape into buns. Place on a buttered baking sheet about an inch apart. Let rise in a warm place until double in bulk — about 1 hour.

Preheat oven to 400°.

Brush tops with the egg slightly beaten with 1 tablespoon of water. Bake in a preheated oven for 20 minutes. After buns have cooled, decorate top of each bun with a cross of Powdered Sugar Icing.

Powdered Sugar Icing

1 egg white

1 cup powdered sugar

1 teaspoon of lemon or orange juice

Place egg white in a small mixing bowl. Beat in 1/4 to 1 cup powdered sugar. Add juice slowly. Drizzle over buns before icing thickens. Makes approximately 24 buns.

James
The Journal
Onboard ship —
Tuesday
Sept 11ᵗʰ, 1951

I just met a neat guy
from the musical department of
NBC in New York
We talked music and radio
Beethoven and Sarnoff
The Philharmonic and the Army
He's shying away from music in the Army same as I-
Sit down to a piano and all they want is "Bumble Boogie"

James
The Journal
Onboard ship —
Sept 11th, 1951
Poem
sung with a gay lilt to
"In the Light of a Moon"

Neckin' on deck in the moonlight
That's the thing to do at sea;
Neckin' on deck in the moonlight
That's the thing for you & me.

The thing that is wrong
With this little song
Is the fact that I have to say
That I'm
Necking alone in the moonlight
With my girl five thousand miles away
(I'm screaming)
My girl's five thousand miles away.

Dough

The first time my mother set my little hands upon a mound of dough to be kneaded, I was in love. Gloria got the idea early on. She wrote to James, "As long as Little Glory gets three meals a day and a few cookies, she's happy. She follows our every move in the kitchen. Loves playing with dough. Loves to learn new things."

My little fingers quickly got the real trick to dough — not too soft and sticky, not too stiff or floury. Flossie always said she could *hear* the proper consistency of dough — she could sense it in her bones and "heah its little dance" on the floured board when it was ready for rising. Imagine you are poking the Pillsbury Doughboy.

James
The Journal
Onboard ship —
Tues Sept 11th, 1951

Loving my family "out loud"
With my officer friends
And worrying about the kids
Forgetting me as a man
Or remembering
Something vague
…a stranger
More with Glory than Martin
She's so little
I'm so depressed
I love you
Make a **Forget-Me-Not-Cake**
And serve it to my children
Tell them their daddy loves them
In every slice

Forget-Me-Not-Cake
(Lemon Pound Cake with Blueberries and Whipped Cream)

3 1/3 cups sugar
10 eggs
1 pound butter, softened
Zest of two lemons (or oranges)
3 tablespoons lemon or orange juice
1 tablespoon vanilla
4 cups sifted flour

Place sugar and eggs in Kitchen Aid or other mixer. Set on medium and mix for ten minutes. Add softened butter and blend well. Slowly add flour, 1/3 at a time, until blended in. Add remaining ingredients and blend until smooth. Pour into well sprayed, high sided cake pan, or Bundt pan, and bake at 350° covered with foil for 30 minutes. Uncover and continue baking for 1 1/4 hours, till firm. Cool or serve warm with berries and cream.

James
The Journal
Onboard ship —
Wed Sept 12th, 1951

The Food onboard *almost* balances the scale
With these Very. Close. Miserable. Quarters.
Hamburger-steak-fries-onions-asparagus
Dreamed of you, but you were two of you:
We were at a Reception — seated at a table
The Band ruffled for a five star general
Who came in the door (it was I)
With a super gorgeous brunette on his arm
In a super sheer black frock (It was you)
You (the brunette) saw me (at the table)
And left me (the general)
Came over to me (at the table)
Looked me in the eye and said
"Dance with me"
Ignoring you (the blonde at the table)…
Before I (at the table) or
You (either of you) could speak,
I (the man) was awake

I dreamed of Glory, too
Awoke in tears

Cloud Biscuits

Every Farm has a biscuit recipe. Gloria added grated cheddar or parmesan cheese; black olives; dried onion; dried parsley. Try finely diced sun dried tomatoes; reduce the amount of milk and add a tablespoon of prepared pesto; grind up a tablespoon of Indian spices such as turmeric, ginger, cumin, mustard seeds and cinnamon and toss into dry ingredients.

    2 cups all-purpose flour
    1 tablespoon sugar
    4 teaspoons baking powder
    1/2 teaspoon salt
    1/2 cup softened butter
    1 beaten egg
    2/3 cup milk*

Sift together dry ingredients. Cut in butter until mixture resembles coarse crumbs. Combine egg and milk; add to flour mixture all at once. Stir until dough follows fork around bowl.

Turn out onto lightly floured surface. Knead gently with heal of hand about 20 strokes. Roll dough to a 3/4 inch thickness. Dip 2 inch biscuit cutter into flour; cut straight down through dough — no twisting. Place on ungreased or parchment covered baking sheet (3/4 inches apart for crusty biscuits, close together for soft sides). If desired, chill 1-3 hours. Bake in a very hot oven (450°) 10 to 14 minutes or till golden brown. Makes about two dozen.

*For drop biscuits, increase milk to 3/4 cup; omit kneading; drop dough from tablespoon onto baking sheet. Proceed as above.

James
The Journal
Onboard ship —
Wed or is it Thurs or… Sept 13th, I think 1951
On the International Dateline
(Attached at the back of the book,
in a copy of the Ship's paper,
is a paragraph entitled, "Dateline"):
*"As the globe of the earth spins along through space,
it turns 360 degrees every 24 hours or 15 degrees
every hour. So, as we travel east, we advance
our clocks one hour for each 15 degrees we travel
— by sea, or air, or land. As we travel west around
the world we would retard our clocks 24 hours.
Where does today begin and yesterday leave off?
The dividing line could be set any place, but the 180th
meridian has been set, out here where there is little
but water and few inhabitants on islands near the meridian.
About midnight tonight we cross the meridian into tomorrow.
Today is Wednesday.
Tomorrow,
on the other side of the 180th meridian,
is Friday.
Sorry, no Thursday this week.
Retard your clocks one hour tonight."*

The Hood

"Can we go with you?" Martin and I chirped in unison as Gloria packed market baskets with breads, jam and butter, and covered them with red checkered cloths. A trip around the neighborhood in the Woodie! We were ecstatic.

Each farm had its own personality: Harmon's "Cobb's Corner" buzzed, clacked and mooed with animal husbandry; the Doolittle's squared-off fields of potatoes, wheat and corn looked like an earth-toned quilt as we bumped and jerked along their gravel lane, careening down the hill to Doolittle Meadows; at the Littlefield's, "Little Fields," everything was verdant with vegetation — every square inch of land covered in the varying greens of broccoli, cabbage and Brussels sprouts. When all this was covered in snow, and the little lakes and ponds were frozen over - a wonderland!

In the back seat of the Woodie, Martin and I tried hopelessly not to squabble over who got to deliver the baskets to the various porches. Gloria preferred to deliver her gifts and go; we wanted to stay and chat a minute; pet ponies; commune with the Animal Kingdom. Once this got started, Gloria was forced to surrender!

Next day, her baskets were returned, left by the Big House kitchen door, filled with bright flowers, warm cheese or fresh dug potatoes, dirt still clinging to the skins.

The Hood in Winter

During the harsh winter, when the power was off or the party-line phones were out, which happened with some regularity, a lot of traipsing around the countryside on snowshoes ensued. If the freezers were draining their preserving ice, the deliveries backed up due to unplowed roads, or someone just couldn't get out, we all took each other stuff — soup, thawing meat, eggs, milk. Slick Johnson's longtime love, Eileen, lived and worked at Doolittle Meadows. If he was gone missing, we checked to see if his snowshoes were missing, too, because, he said, "Sure as shootin', I'll be on my way over t' there to help her out." When we were snowed in because the one mile "Sugar Lane" couldn't be plowed, Martin's friend Jason's mother hiked in with his homework!

James
The Journal
Onboard ship —
Sept 14th, 1951

Tonight I pondered the need of letters
With my closest onboard buddies…
Is it better to get daily "duty" letters? or
Is it more desirable to wait for longer, substantial ones?
We laughed at ourselves
For being too blue to pursue these thoughts
And thinking of them in the first place!
The wind is 60 miles an hour
With roaring billows — and an up and down ship
The storm is passing — still, the ship is tossing
My stomach is not so affected
I must be a sailor now! Ha!
Get it straight, though —
I have no desire ever to go to sea again
Me, for plane travel whenever possible
Better still — load my family in the Woodie and go!
10,000 words could not say
How much I love you…

There was an Initiation tonight
Of first time Crossers of
The International Date Line —
I am exempted since
I have previously crossed the Equator

Some were dunked in flour
The hose was turned on some
Egg massages for others!
All were made to
Kiss the big toe of King Neptune...

Fleecy clouds today

Sourdough

Ew! What is that?" I asked, noticing the burbling glop in the jar in the fridge.

"Sourdough Starter," Gloria said, as she took it out, removed some of the glop from the jar, added some other stuff to it and put it back.

"Why did you do that?" I asked.

"You have to feed it," she said.

"Ew! It's *alive*?"

In a spring-top jar on the top shelf of the refrigerator was Gloria's prized, seven year old **Sourdough Starter,** a wedding gift from a San Francisco girlfriend. **Sourdough Starter:** a creature that lived in the fridge that had to be fed once a week! Sourdough likely originated around 1500 BC, in Egypt, and was the first form of leavening historically noted. Throughout the Middle Ages, Sourdough leavened most bread, then was replaced by the barm from beer brewing and then later cultured yeast.

The creature in the fridge is a batter of flour and water, filled with living yeast and bacteria, which form a stable symbiotic relationship, creating a little tribe of microorganisms, and, with proper care and feeding, and very short walks from fridge to counter and back to fridge, can live for eons. I named our Sourdough Starter **Fred**. In a Cub Scouts craft class, Martin made a 12 inch woven plastic leash which he hung around the top of the jar.

Blend a cup of warm water and a cup of flour, and pour it into a clean, wide-mouthed glass jar with a rubber seal: or a crock with a loose lid; plastic containers are OK, but not ideal. They're *plastic*. Metallic containers are chemically reactive and would probably turn your starter to some other science experiment (for the same reason, avoid using metal utensils to stir your starter).

That's it, Darlin'. You can add a little commercial yeast to a **Starter** to give it a boost and make it lighter, but sourdough snobs frown on this. And, **Starter** made with commercial yeast produces less distinctive sour flavor than the real thing. Experiment! Try this, birth your own.

Sourdough Starter has to be kept warm to propagate, so experienced miners and settlers in California carried a well-guarded pouch of starter either around their neck or on a belt inside their pants. **Sourdough Bread** became so common during the Northern California Gold Rush, that "Sourdough" became a general nickname for the gold prospectors, and "Sourdough Sam" still reigns supreme as the mascot of the San Francisco 49ers.

To make **Sourdough Bread**, remove some of the **Starter** from your container and blend it with some flour to make dough, always adding something back to the container. The yeast propagates, and leavens your bread in its own gaseous way.

James
The Journal
Onboard ship —
Sun Sept 16th, 1951

The Sea is Calm today
And I slept well
Although these 6" wide planks
These narrow bunks
These tiny so-called beds
Were made for smaller men

James
The Journal
Onboard ship —

The Sea

Just a little touch of it
Not so goddam much of it
Would have been enough of it
The never-ending sea

While there is a lot of it
We should learn the plot of it
Why there's such a pot of it
The ever-lasting sea

Why would any thinking man
Step his foot away from land
Willing to forsake his sand
For the stretching sea

Certainly if I had the choice
If they'd asked, I'd have a voice
To tell them it could not be woise!
The lousy pretty sea

When at last I do return
To that home for which I yearn
Boats like this I will but spurn
To cross the big old sea
Give me a plane, yes fly me home
And there I'll rest my balding dome
Away from the beautiful sea

Feed Your Creature

For three or four days, keep your **Fred** in a warm place; 70-80 degrees, no hotter than 100! High temperature will kill your little budding blob. The yeast already in the flour will grow quickly under these conditions. To feed the **Starter**, discard half of it and add a half-cup of flour and a half-cup of water, every 24 hours. It will form a liquid on top with a truly enchanting fragrance (especially if you like beer) which is called **Hooch,** an alcoholic froth, which, according to legend, is shortened from the Tlingit *Hootchinoo,* the name of an Alaskan indigenous tribe that distilled some kind of liquor. It is what makes sourdough *sour* dough! When the **Hooch** forms, you have achieved **Sourdough Starter**. Mix it back in. Keep the starter in your fridge, with a loose lid on it - allow it to breath. Feed it once a week, or so. If you enjoy anthropomorphizing microorganisms, be sure to name your Creature.

Proofing the Sponge

Before you make dough, begin with a sponge, a fermented batter. Pour 2 cups of **Sourdough Starter** into a large glass or ceramic bowl. Warming the bowl for few minutes with warm water helps create the proper environment.

Add a cup of warm water and a cup of flour to the bowl. Stir well, and set it in a warm place for several hours. This is called "proofing," or fermenting. The longer you proof the sponge, the more sour the flavor. The batter may be used for pancakes, waffles, muffins, bread or cake. The proofing-time varies, but setting your sponge out to proof overnight is great.

When using in a recipe, or sharing with a friend, take 2 cups starter out and add more flour and water to your **Starter**.

Sourdough Bread

2 cups of sponge from your proofed starter
3 cups of unbleached flour
2 tablespoons of oil (or softened butter)
4 teaspoons of sugar
2 teaspoons of salt

To the sponge, add the sugar, salt, and oil (the oil is optional - you can use softened butter instead, or no oil at all). Knead in enough flour about a half cup at a time to make nice, springy bread dough. Remember that flour amounts are approximate — when you get that "feel," stop adding flour.

Let the dough rise in a warm place, in a bowl covered loosely with a towel. Sourdough rises more slowly than yeast bread, about an hour or so. Let it double in bulk. When it is soft and springy to the touch, punch the dough down and knead a little more. Make a loaf shape and place it on a baking sheet (lightly greased or sprinkled with cornmeal). Or place in a sprayed loaf pan. Slit the top if you like, and cover the loaf with a towel and place it in a warm place to rise again, until doubled in bulk.

Place the pan with the loaf in your oven, and then turn your oven to 350° and bake the bread for 30-45 minutes. *Do not preheat the oven*. The loaf is done when the crust is brown and the bottom sounds hollow when thumped with your thumb. Turn the loaf out onto a cooling rack or a towel and let it cool for an hour before slicing.

James
The Journal
Onboard ship —
Mon Sept 17th, 1951

Two days more!
We are actually focused
On what uniforms to wear upon landing!
What excitement!
735 choices for assignments!
Most likely, I'll be an assistant to a general
Less likely — Bandleader
Can't handle any more of the movies shown onboard
Movies to me:
A thermos of coffee,
A drive-in,
My little family
I've been afraid to tackle
Telling you how much I love you
Hesitate to break down
In front of men in close quarters
But, they are all feeling the same way

Sourdough Onion Bread

Gloria, true to her era, was big on Lipton Onion Soup Mix. She made pot roast with it, the ubiquitous Onion Dip, Bread — everything but onion soup! That she made from scratch.

2 tablespoons sugar
1 teaspoon salt
3 tablespoons butter, melted and cooled
1 envelope onion soup mix
About 3 cups all-purpose flour

To 2 cups starter, add sugar, salt, butter, onion soup mix and enough flour to make a soft dough. Knead on floured board until smooth, about 15 minutes. Place in oiled bowl turning the dough once to oil all sides. Cover and let rise in warm place until doubled in bulk, about 1 1/4 hours.

Punch down. Let rest 15 minutes and shape into loaf. Place in oiled 9 x 5 inch loaf pan or 1 quart oven proof bowl. Cover and let rise until doubled in bulk — about 1 hour.

Bake at 375° about 50 minutes. Makes 1 loaf.

James
The Journal
Onboard ship —
Tues Sept 18th, 1951

Every couple of nights,
We turn the clocks back an hour
We go to bed at 11
Wake up at 7
Turn clock to 6
We are...
Lemme see...
12 hours behind you
Or ten ahead...
No ten... — oh, the heck with it
The Sea is tranquil
A biiiiig, flat lake
I am ready to Get. Off. This. Boat.
Oh, my Gloria.

Refrigerator Rolls

Gloria loved this bread, because you could make the dough in the morning and forget about it until about 5. Meanwhile, she'd clean house, make curtains, knit socks, paint walls and help mend fences.

3 1/2 dozen

Mix:
1 1/2 cups lukewarm water
1/2 cup sugar
1 1/2 teaspoons salt
Dissolve 2 packets dry yeast in mixture
Stir in:
1 egg
1/4 cup soft butter

Mix in:

6-7 cups sifted all-purpose flour

Place in oiled bowl, turning once to cover dough in oil on all surfaces. Cover tightly with waxed paper and damp cloth. Keep in refrigerator until ready to use, up to six hours. Shape into rolls and cover with damp cloth. Let rise for 1 1/2- 2 hours. Bake at 400° for 12-15 minutes.

James
The Journal
Onboard ship —
Wed Sept 19th, 1951

On Okinawa now
Looks like Korea for me
More tomorrow

Ups...

Pop, SugarPop, Mr. Upsy & Downsy, would flash me a big grin and say, "Hello, Little Darlin', come, let's ride the fat little ponies," and off we'd tear on a romp around the estate — him on a tubby, genial chestnut mare named, don't ask me why, Firenose, and me on Molly, a shaggy, aging, plump, slow and therefore perfect palomino pony. These excursions were luscious with Pop's bright cold light, his luminosity— just poking our noses in old sheds and meandering along fence-lines, looking for breaks the sheep might wiggle through, was made magical by his colorful running commentary and glossy presence. If we brought lunch, even better!

Watching me munch a wheat bread and banana sandwich while plodding along on Molly's wide back, he began a discourse on bread: "Man first lived on seeds, you know — and made the first attempt at bread by grinding it up and adding water, baking it in the sun. Then they moved on to acorns and nuts. Later, they added dried fruit and when they discovered fire, they'd bake it in the coals and it became pemmican, the first bread known to man."

Farm Animals

Have I not told you about the two sheep and the goat? Myrtle, Greta and Git. They had the run of the place, munching on the grasses, wandering the estate at will. Pop fenced them inside 200 acres. Lincoln fenced them out of his garden with equal enthusiasm.

For at least a year, Herman, the boldly pushy 30 pound, white Norwegian goose, sported a faded and wilted red bow around his neck that one of the boys tied on for a joke, but then could never get close enough to Herman again to take it off. Herman chased me up the sloping side of Major's large, German Shepherd-sized dog house to its little roof, where I teetered for several hours, or so it seemed, until Pop gently lifted me down. Herman made a honking great racket announcing visitors, which Pop liked. Pop said Major was too dignified for noisy announcing. His 6 years as an Army Pooch gave him airs, he said, and, in retirement, would not lower himself to bark at just any old thing.

On the backs of our meandering ponies, we devised good travel sandwiches: cream cheese laced with black olives and chopped walnuts; grated orange rind, chopped pecans and cream cheese on **Apricot Bread**; crushed hardboiled egg and bacon mixed with mayonnaise and mustard; mushed deviled eggs with thinly sliced cucumbers on pumpernickel; layered deviled eggs with tuna and watercress. Peanut butter and orange marmalade on wheat bread with raisins.

Sugar Land

On a ride up the Kickapoo Mound, sandwiches in our knapsacks, Pop launched in to a discourse on salesmanship.

Sometimes, he talked so much he irritated his vocal chords. This was one of those times. "GloryDarlin'," he rasped... "Did you know how this whole Sugar Department Store business got started?"

I knew I was in for a long, enlightening story.

"I did not just jump into department store land willy-nilly. No. I started by selling women's face powder door to door."

"Who made it for you?"

"I did! Can you believe it? In my basement, like a cook or a chemist, even an artist, I mixed powdered colors with corn starch and called it face powder, put a scoop into a brown paper bag on which I had written "SugarFace" and began walking the neighborhood, since I was currently without the good services of a car. It was in the 20s, when cosmetics were scarce and money scarcer. I made 10 bucks the first day. And it was not just my winning personality!" He smiled, broadly.

"What was it?" I dutifully asked.

"Well," he said, settling into his story, "salesmanship is a combination of things. I wasn't selling a cosmetic. I was selling pretty, healthy-looking skin. You've got to have the right words, and *believe* in what you are selling."

"And what about SugarShave? Did you make that, too?"

"Ahh, no. My friend, Ernest Blok, the out-of-work real-life chemist down the road, he made that. He ran his hands through his mop of crazy white hair while experimenting, and cured his dandruff! I bought the formula lickety-split and made it SugarShave, an all-around remedy for skin, shaving and cleansing. Made my fortune right there, I did. The Sugar Department Store just kind of grew up around it."

Apricot Bread

Soak in warm water 30 minutes...1 cup chopped dried apricots*

Drain and chop apricots into small bits.

Mix ....1 cup sugar

2 tablespoons softened butter

1 egg

Stir in....1/4 cup water

1/2 cup orange juice

Sift together...2 cups flour

2 teaspoons baking powder

1/4 teaspoon baking soda

1 teaspoon salt

Mix sifted ingredients with wet ingredients. Add apricots (and chopped nuts if desired). Line bottom of an oiled or sprayed loaf pan with parchment. Pour in batter. Let stand 20 minutes. Bake at 350° 55-65 minutes.

*The apricots can be soaked in warm rum or brandy for a treat

And Downs...

And then, out of the blue, Pop buried himself in green quilts and blankies in the high, canopied bed upstairs and was unseen for weeks.

"What's up with SugarPop?" I asked.

"The old trouble," Marnie sighed in her mildly frenchified voice. He was a big, dramatic guy, and she had many euphemisms for his swinging moods. The Old Trouble. Beneath-the-Sheets. Upsy. Downsy. Take-to-the-Bed.

During an extreme, the kids were sheltered (he tended to be blindly uncontrollable if he crashed through the house during a dizzy spell) and Marnie hid the checkbook and the keys.

Pop's "man," Mr. Talbot: chauffeur, valet, beloved family retainer, sat on a chair outside the bedroom door at the top of the curving mahogany stairs at these times, protecting the ailing man *beneath-the-sheets* in the darkened room from intruders. "Jest helpin' Mr. Suga' to stay in 'de bed till he get bettah."

Mr. Talbot - hair black as night, bundled under a natty leather cap. His jacket, a hand-me-down-from-Pop-I'm-sure-tweed, sported suede elbow patches. He smoked a pipe, out on the screened-in porch that ran the length of the backside of the Big House, facing the main paddock and an old, crumbling river-stone barbeque.

Mr. Talbot was shot and killed some years later in a barroom fight over a hooker, whose honor he was protecting. My appreciation of Mr. Talbot increased no end when I learned this fact in my teens.

I didn't know his first name until then, either, although he sat with Martin and me and our cousins many nights on the back porch — our fave babysitter. Jimmy. Jimmy Talbot. Mr. Talbot.

Gloria's remedy for Pop's "trouble," of course, was nourishing, hot food.

There was nothing in life that couldn't be fixed, or at least improved, and for a moment ignored, by warm rolls and a hot cup of strong, black tea or a bowl of **Chicken Soup**. SugarPop took Gloria's ministrations with dark or glittering good grace, depending, coddled by Mr. Talbot and supported by the long-suffering Marnie.

I remember a chat we had years later about the whole idea of chicken soup and its curative properties. Gloria said, "It's not really the chicken, or the broth, although they have nutrients and all that. It's you, the maker, the cook. You put your *self* in Chicken Soup, you know? Pray in it, if you like. That's what tenderizes the moment."

Flossie's Special Chicken Soup

1/4 cup olive oil

1 onion, chopped

2 cloves garlic, chopped

1/2 cup celery, chopped

6 carrots, peeled and chopped

6 white potatoes, cut in bite sized pieces

1 tablespoon salt

1/4 teaspoon pepper

4 quarts Dark or Clear Chicken Stock

6 tomatoes, coarsely chopped

1 whole cooked chicken, pieces pulled

6 tablespoons chopped fresh parsley

Add other herbs at will (thyme, oregano, rosemary, sage)

In a large pot, sauté vegetables in hot olive oil about 5 minutes, stirring frequently. Add stock, bring to simmer. Cook 15 minutes. Add chicken pieces. Turn off heat until ready to serve. Add parsley before serving. You can omit the potatoes and serve the soup over thin pasta. Or you can leave out the chicken, add pesto and call it **Minestrone**. As with everything, add love.

James
The Journal
Fri Sept 21st, 1951

On Japanese train now
Bound for another processing point
Where am I going?

Golden Crescents

These were Pop's favorites, an Americanized version of a French Croissant, which take about ten times as long to make and contain about three times the amount of butter. A Golden Crescent does have the same shape, just not the flakiness. Think: good, quick rolls in a quarter-moon shape.

Beat with rotary mixer until smooth:
1/2 cup sugar
1/2 cup soft butter
1 teaspoon salt
2 eggs

Stir in:
3/4 cup lukewarm milk
2 packages yeast (dissolved in the milk)

Mix in with spoon:
4 cups sifted flour

Scrape down dough from sides of bowl. Cover with damp cloth and let rise till double — about 1 1/2 hours. Divide dough into two parts. Roll each into circle about 1/4 inch thick and 16 inches diameter. Cut each circle into 16 pie wedges. Roll up each piece so that the long point winds up on the outside. Stretch each roll gently into crescent shape. Cover with damp cloth and let rise about one hour. Bake 10-15 minutes at 400°. Brush with soft butter.

Keeping a depressed manic-depressive in bed and out of trouble and a manic manic-depressive from spending all his money and out of trouble was a full time job for Marnie. Covering for Pop kept her out of the kitchen, which was good: she threw Flossie off her game when she meddled with the system. Our Marnie wasn't much of a cook — she burnt pots and smoked up the kitchen. She used salt instead of sugar in a cake once. Her best contribution to sustenance was creating a menu for dinner; she knew how to order things. Themes were a specialty, like Gloria's **Chinese Beef and Onions** served with rice and stir-fried vegetables.

Chinese Beef and Onions

1 pound sirloin, cut in 1/4" x 1" x 2" strips
cut across the grain

Salt and pepper
2 tablespoon rice wine
or dry sherry
1 teaspoon sesame oil
1 tablespoon cornstarch

1 tablespoon flour
2 medium red or white onions, thinly sliced
1 clove garlic, crushed
2 slices ginger,
peeled and crushed
2 green onions,
cut in 1" pieces

3 tablespoons dark soy sauce
2 tablespoon rice wine
or dry sherry
4 tablespoons oil for
stir-frying

Mix the first four ingredients in a bowl and marinate the beef for 15 - 20 minutes.

Heat the wok. Add 2 tablespoons oil, coating the sides of the wok. Pat the beef dry, dredge in flour and add to hot oil. Brown and remove from wok.

Add a bit more oil to the wok. Add ginger and garlic. Stir-fry for 30 seconds. Add the onions and stir-fry until softened.

Stir in soy sauce, rice wine or sherry, and sugar. Add the beef back to the wok. Stir in the green onion. Sprinkle with sesame oil and toss lightly. Serve hot over rice.

The French

Marnie was the youngest of eight children of French immigrants, who managed a little farmette and family business in Kansas. The Tourniers immigrated to the United States when Maria Monique (our Marnie) was quite young, so her soft and fluttery voice bore just a trace of accent. When she answered the phone, she didn't say "Hello," or "The Sugar Farm." Marnie pinched the receiver between two fingers, as if it smelled bad or would bite, dangling it next to her ear and fluting, "Y-e-ssss," turning the word into three warm syllables reminiscent of the Good Witch Glenda.

She took good care of Pop, though, as long as she could. And that man was a sack of cats.

Cheese Straws

If I gave **Cheese Straws** to Marnie, she rewarded me with her Mona Lisa smile — lips thinly pressed together in an encyclopedia of emotion... and a little weariness creased into the edges. She nibbled **Cheese Straws** and played cards with the four cousins - Crazy Eights and Fish - to pass her lonely days while Pop slept off his mad dreams and short circuits. She was protective of him — *and* her elegant hands, soft from non-use and gentle care; long, oval nails, bright shiny red, at the ends of fingers covered in mildly gaudy diamond rings. She boasted that she'd never washed a dish in her life. At 4, I was already a skeptic. I couldn't imagine anyone not washing dishes, especially in a family of 10 on a farm in Kansas.

Cheese Straws
1/2 cup sifted all-purpose flour
Dash salt
2 oz. gruyere cheese, shredded
3 oz. cream cheese
1/4 cup butter
1 egg yolk
2 tablespoons water

Preheat oven to 375°. Sift flour and salt together in mixing bowl. Cut both kinds of cheese into flour mixture with pastry blender or fork until mixture looks mealy. Then work the dough gently with your hands until it holds together in a mass.

Roll 1/8 inch thick on a lightly floured surface and cut into thin rectangles about 3 x 1/2 inches in size. Place on baking sheet, brush with mixture of egg yolk and water and sprinkle tops with coarse salt, caraway seeds or poppy seeds. Bake 10-12 minutes. Makes lots.

Great with a cup of hot boullion.
Perfect with salads.
Delicious as appetizers.
Good for grandmothers.

Mama T

Marnie's mother, Mama T, Madame la Tournier, was renowned as a cook, I hear. I never met her, but I found this method for **Brioche** scrawled on a card with her signature, Celine, tucked in one of Gloria's Red Binders. These techniques in the script of the departed are icons of history. I could research this recipe online, or flip though a cookbook, but a few minutes with this old stained card in my hands conjured up a picture of Mama T in the kitchen:

An ample-and-low-bosomed Amazon of a lady in a red and grey calico dress, Peter Pan collar around her awesome neck, and a big, white apron flopped over her bountiful front; solid legs and feet, in sensible black shoes; dark hair wiry and sprinkled with grey, hobbed into a low, loose ponytail at the nape of her neck with a red bow haphazardly tied, ribbons dangling. While she beats her Brioche batter with a wooden spoon, Mama T is in mild despair over her youngest daughter's kitchen idiocy. "Nothing to be done, I z'pose," she mumbles to herself through full French lips. "Six girls, and only one of z'em inept in ze kitchen. Pas mal."

Braided Brioche

1 3/4 - 2 1/4 un-sifted flour
1/4 cup sugar
3/4 teaspoon salt
1 package active dry yeast
1/4 cup milk
1/4 cup water
1/3 cup butter
2 eggs
1/2 teaspoon lemon juice
Melted butter
1 egg white
1 tablespoon sugar

Mix 3/4 cup flour, sugar and un-dissolved yeast in a large mixing bowl.

Combine milk, water and 1/4 cup butter in a saucepan. Heat slowly until the combined ingredients are lukewarm. Gradually add to dry ingredients and beat two minutes at medium speed with electric mixer, scraping bowl occasionally. Add eggs, lemon and 1/2 cup or enough flour to make a thick batter or sponge. Beat at high speed two minutes, scraping bowl occasionally. Stir in enough additional batter to make a stiff batter. Beat by hand five minutes. Brush top of dough with melted butter. Cover and let rise in warm place free of draft until doubled in bulk, about 1 hour.

Stir batter down; cover tightly with foil and refrigerate overnight.

Turn out onto heavily floured surface. Divide into three pieces; roll each piece into a 10 inch log. Braid the logs together; pinch ends to seal. Place in oiled or sprayed 8 inch loaf pan. Cover and let rise in a warm place until doubled in bulk, about 1 hour.

Combine egg white and 1 tablespoon sugar. Brush loaf. Bake at 375° for about 30 minutes or until done (when an inserted knife comes out clean!) Remove from pan and cool on wire rack.

Brioche A Tete

Brioche dates back to the 15th century. It is rich in eggs and butter. The sugared egg wash caramelizes and forms a lovely brown crust. Brioche a Tete is the same dough as above, only smaller, with a little topknot or hat (literally, "head").

Prepare dough as directed for loaf. Remove from refrigerator. Turn out onto heavily floured board. Divide into 2 pieces — one 3/4 piece, one 1/4 piece. Cut larger piece into twelve equal pieces. Form into smooth balls. Place in well-oiled or sprayed muffin pan. Cut smaller pieces into twelve equal pieces. Form into smooth balls. Dampen slightly with cold water. Press a small ball into the top of each of the larger pieces in the muffin pan. Cover and let rise in a warm place until doubled in bulk, about an hour. Brush on egg white and sugar combination. Bake at 375° for about 15-20 minutes, or until golden. Remove from pan and cool on wire rack.

James
The Journal
Sat 22nd, 1951

In Sasebo
30 hours on the train
No assignment yet
Sasebo is much like
Yokohama and Hiroshima — gray
Such small people-
Sleepers, chairs,
Toilets designed for them
Not us!
Flush toilets are rare among common people
No paved roads
Driving on the left
People tinkle in the streets!
I'm well and fit
No assignment yet

So much for this book
Will close to send it now
I love you, more dearly than ever
And miss you more than I can describe
My heart is with my family
And I love you all so much

End of journal

Freaked!

Only once in all the years I knew Pop, who died in 1972, did I ever experience one of his "downsies" up-close and personal; his wife, children and retainers were that good at protecting him and sheltering the next generation. During the highs, the significance of which I did not grasp at the time, we spent many hours together, since the Farm was his safe-haven, and I his little buddy, his partner on ponies. During the lows, he dove Beneath-the-Sheets, protected — once electro-shocked. The highs were more manageable if they could keep him on the Farm and entertained during his periods of expansive philanthropy. Once, when someone admired his new car, he handed them the keys and said, "It's yours!" This was typical. Bless his heart.

Who knew I was an accomplice for his well-being? I just enjoyed the company of this brightly lit talker, even after James returned home and went head-to-head with Pop too many times for his own good.

In their city-house, near Cleveland, Pop and Marnie lived during the week, or when Pop went to his office. T and I were visiting, excited to be on our own for an adventure, without all the parents. Ellen, the city-housekeeper, brought us breakfast in bed. We lounged on the lavender chenille spread on the double bed we shared, like princesses, with a tray of hot chocolate in mugs, **Messed-Up Eggs** and cinnamon "toast points."

Marnie took us shopping and then for lunch at Stouffer's. We wore polka dotted dresses with wide belts tied in bows at the back, perky little felt hats, white gloves, black patent leather shoes and white anklets trimmed with lace, and camel hair coats. We carried mini black patent leather handbags with brass snaps, in which we stuffed our hankies and scrunched-up dollar bills. We did this.

We paraded in our new pink quilted robes that evening in a before-bed-time fashion show for Pop, who peered at us over the top of his newspaper with a scowl I had never seen before.

"SugarPop!" I said, just not *getting* how this might set him off. "Come with us outside while we see how cold it is in our quilty pink robes!" We dashed out the front door.

Throwing down his paper in a pique, he chased us outside, yelling:

"What the Sam Hill do you think you're doing, going outside in your nightclothes? Get back inside, you danged little trollops, before I ...."

Reaching for me, he slipped on the icy sidewalk and fell.

Pop had this strange look in his eyes, like he didn't really see me; he was looking at something just beyond me. I froze in place, shocked. T looked like she'd seen a green four-headed monster from Mars.

Oh my.

Mr. Talbot jumped out of his chair in the quiet kitchen to intervene, dashing out into the snow to Pop's side.

"Mr. Suga', honey, now come 'dis way," Mr. Talbot said in his soft, tender voice, taking Pop's arm in a firm grasp. "Let's you 'n me go inside for a little warm drink."

Pop looked dazed, like he didn't know where he was. He let Mr. Talbot take him in and up the stairs.

Marnie gathered us up in her arms, saying, "There, there, it's all right. Your Pop'z just not himself tonight."

She asked Ellen for a **Posset** for "Upstairs" and some **Sour Cream Buns** for us.

Messed-Up Eggs

Heat a pat of butter in a frying pan until it browns. Add several eggs, as if you were making them sunny side up. When the whites begin to brown around the edges, and are almost done but the yolk still soft in the middle, mess them up with a fork to lightly scramble and serve immediately. Not really scrambled eggs, where everything turns yellow — **Messed-Up Eggs** maintain a little integrity between the yolks and the whites. Salt to taste.

Sour Cream Buns

Heat to lukewarm in large saucepan …1 cup sour cream*
Remove from heat.
Stir until well blended ….2 tablespoons butter
3 tablespoons sugar
1/8 teaspoon soda
1 teaspoon salt
Add …1 large egg
1 package yeast
Stir until yeast dissolves.
Mix in …3 cups flour

Turn out onto lightly floured board. Knead lightly a few seconds to form a smooth ball. Cover with damp cloth and let stand ten minutes to tighten up. Roll out dough ¼ inch thick into a rectangle 6" x 24".

Spread with ....2 tablespoons soft butter
Sprinkle with ...1/3 cup brown sugar
1 teaspoon cinnamon

Roll up, beginning at wide end. Seal well by pinching edges of dough into roll. Cut into 12 slices about 1 1/2 inch thick. Place in oiled or sprayed muffin cups. Cover with damp cloth and set to rise in a warm place about one hour.

Bake 12-15 minutes at 375°. While still warm, ice with confectioner's sugar icing.

*To sour sweet cream, measure 1 tablespoon lemon juice or vinegar into measuring cup. Fill to one cup level with sweet cream.

Backstairs

Flossie squeezed her donut round body onto the oak bench beside me at the kitchen table. We sat in the quiet, puzzling over my latest paper doll dress design. She wafted a general sugar-like fragrance and her ample bosom and hips, wrapped-up tight in a black uniform with white eyelet collars, filled the space. Her black frizzy curls were stuffed inside a turban white as snow. Flossie ironed a starched white eyelet trimmed apron, fresh every morning. When tired or blue or sick, I lay my head in her soft springy lap.

Bessie and Lincoln, on the other hand, were rail thin; Flossie called them X-ray One and Two.

We watched, Flossie and I, while, Bessie, humming, minded her business in the Big Pantry, an alcove with an accordion door, shelves and a little antique desk inside. She sorted this and that, carefully preparing labels for the glass jars in neat, square printing, copied a few new recipes into the Big House Book. Cinnamon and spice lingered on Bessie's skin. Sleek black hair and high cheekbones gave her a haughty Indian half-breed look, or so La Muse declared.

"Punch down 'dat dough, please, will you, Bess?" Flossie asked, as she re-drew a line for me. "Dis girl's Sweet Dough gotta be ready now."

60 Minute Sweet Dough

Heat to lukewarm in medium sized saucepan….1/2 cup milk
Remove from heat.
Stir in…1 teaspoon salt
1 tablespoon sugar1 package dry yeast
Stir until yeast is dissolved.
Mix in …1 egg
2 tablespoons soft butter
Mix in (just enough to handle easily)….2- 2 1/4 sifted flour

Mix dough with hand in bowl until moderately stiff. Turn onto floured board and knead several times. Shape as directed below. Cover with damp cloth and let rise in warm place until almost double in bulk — 35-40 minutes.

Bake 20-25 minutes in 400° oven until golden brown. Serve immediately.

Cinnamon Swirls

Roll out dough into a rectangle 12" x 7". Spread surface with 1 tablespoon soft butter. Sprinkle with sugar or brown sugar and cinnamon. Roll up beginning at wide end. Seal tightly by pinching the edges of dough into roll. Cut into 12 slices. Place cut-side-down with a little space in between in an oiled or sprayed 9 inch round pan or in a circle on a baking sheet. After baking, if desired, mix 1 cup confectioner's sugar with 1/3 cup orange juice and pour over warm rolls before serving.

Pecan Rolls

Make as for Cinnamon Swirls above — except, place cut slices in a pan that has been coated with 1/4 cup each melted butter, brown sugar and chopped pecans. When baked, turn pan upside down onto platter.

Lincoln and Flossie…

Well. He arrived at the back-door, his long lanky arms filled with spring garden and field flowers, and presented them to her as if they were long stemmed roses wrapped with colored cellophane and red ribbon. Flossie brayed like a donkey, and then giggled, her big girdled body wiggling, and took the flowers as if she were Miss America accepting her due reward. Lincoln said, "Wife! You are the beatenest!" That's how I remember them.

In the Big House, Lincoln magically appeared at table-side in crisp white shirts and black pants - in the garden, his patched denim overalls were rolled up above his ankles, his slender feet bare and covered with dirt.

Backstairs was off-limits. Gloria and Marnie thought it only right that Flossie, Bessie and Lincoln have some privacy.

We longed to go, though. Their rooms were neat and simple, with highly polished wood floors, chenille bedcovers and big colorful braided rag rugs.

Lincoln's rugs were prized by the family, envied by the neighbors. Limited as he was by winter weather, he accumulated a little extra cash by taking in old cotton clothes to tear into strips, braid and hand-sew into rugs, creating beauty out of the neighborhood rag bags.

In late evening, after chores were done, dishes washed, the "Folks" put to bed with their **Possets** or **Toddies** or hot water bottles, Flossie, Bessie and Lincoln murmured and laughed in the kitchen, playing cards or dominoes, sharing a little gossip before going up the Backstairs to their rooms. In winter, cotton fibers filled the air.

Hot Toddy

A sore throat, cold or flu "calmer"

1 cup boiling water
1/4 cup brandy
1 tablespoon honey
juice of one lemon
cinnamon stick, optional

While boiling the water, place other ingredients in large cup. Pour in hot water. Steep a few minutes. Enjoy while warm. (Ingredients can be doubled and kept warm in a thermos).

A Good Posset
1 cup milk, scalded
Pinch each: cinnamon, cardamom, nutmeg, salt
sugar or honey, optional

Serve in a beautiful cup or mug. Sprinkle with sweet cocoa powder or cinnamon.

As in all families, some kind of adult-troubling, Toddy or Posset-needing drama lurked behind the potted plants: Pop's swinging moods, Marnie's worry over Pop's moods, business debacles that were likely the fallout from Pop's moods, horse talk, missing husbands, sick cousins. But, something warm and comforting could always be found in the kitchen. Somewhat driven by necessity, more pressed by her own private pain and need, Gloria endeavored to nourish the 15 or so souls in her care.

She was my own little Food Network: no demanding chefs, no competitions — just a generous portion of Love added into every great recipe.

And, I? Her little audience of one, an avid mini cook-to-be.

James
Sat Sept 22nd

I await word from home

Stock

Mostly stress-free (I was four!), I thought the Farm fabulous, even in snow. I knew little of horses, except Molly, any family drama was over my head and, much as I loved Pop, the Sugar Department Store was on Pluto… I was busy making paper doll clothes and learning the art of a good soup stock.

"HoneyDarlin'," Flossie said, "Scrape these heah carrots — always have carrots, onions and cel'ry — then add whatevah else you want."

When I started rubbing white-jacketed elbows with chefs, I discovered that by instinct, Flossie had been preparing a good mirepoix, supposedly named after C. P. G. F. (Charles Pierre Gaston François) de Lévis, duke of Mirepoix, whose ancestors had been lords of Mirepoix in Languedoc since the eleventh century.

C.P.G.F. was himself an 18th-century marechel, or marshal, of France and an ambassador for the French King, Louis XV. Lord Mirepoix's *chef de cuisine* established those three sautéed vegetables as the basis for his own culinary craft, and called it a *mirepoix* in honor of his not-so-illustrious patron.

As culinary legends go, this one disses the hapless Duke of Mirepoix as an apparently incompetent and mediocre guy… and who owed his great wealth to the deep… uhm… affection Louis XV felt toward his wife. Alas, he really had but one other claim to fame: his name became a base for a sauce.

Today, I keep the bones from Roasted Chickens (my own, or Whole Foods!) in plastic Zip Locks in the freezer until I have 5 or 6. Then I throw them in the pot with a good mirepoix, make enough stock to fill 8 or 12 plastic quart containers and keep them in the freezer. Or, reduce it down for a couple of extra hours, cool it, and pour into ice cube trays and freeze. When frozen, remove from trays and place cubes in a plastic bag. Keep in the freezer for sauces.

Roast Chicken
Preheat the oven to 450°.

One 2- to 3-pound organic chicken
Kosher salt and freshly ground black pepper
2 teaspoons minced thyme, rosemary, oregano and or tarragon

Rinse the chicken and dry it very well with paper towels, inside and out.

Salt and pepper the cavity, then truss the bird. Trussing the chicken helps to cook it evenly, and it also makes for a more beautiful roasted bird.

Salt the chicken so that it has a nice uniform coating that will result in a crisp, salty, flavorful skin (about 1 tablespoon). Season to taste with pepper.

Place the chicken in roasting pan and put it in the oven. Turn oven down to 350º and roast 60-90 minutes. Remove it from the oven. Baste the chicken with the juices and herbs and let stand for 15 minutes on a cutting board.

Remove the twine. I like to "pull" the meat from the bones rather than slicing it away, so I let it cool enough to get my washed fingers into the hard to reach places. If you are serving the meat, reserve the pieces in individual portions. If using for salad or soup, shred or pull it to small pieces. Save those bones.

James
Sept. 28:

Hey —
I've finally gotten assigned
And it's a good job
Chief Clerk and Assistant
To the General in Charge of Personnel.
Yes, Korea.
Details later

James
Sept 28th

The Assignment system is a bit of a joke here
We were passed through five assignment centers
Five bus rides
To get here — really
To a "replacement company"
Which receives us (officers)
And passes us along …
To the next assignment center!
We are laughing — an old story, this is
BUT!
I was interviewed by a sensible officer —
Who is keeping me
To work for him in his office
I'll be Assistant to the G-1…
So, compare a division
To a corporation
General = President
Chief of Staff= VP & General Mgr.
Four Asst Chiefs of Staff = VPs
G-1=personnel, G-2=intelligence, G-3=operations, G-4=supply
G's are policy level groups of the division
They establish plans and policies regarding operations
For your immediate relief of mind,
We are never on the fighting line
We are 35 miles from any shooting

I'll be Chief Clerk and Secretary
To the VP in Charge of Personnel
Who makes decisions regarding
Assignments:
Relief, transfer, shuffling
I receive credit for four months
For each one month I serve here!
Six months in this spot
Equals my commitment
To 2 years in the Far East!

James
Sept 28th, 1951 later

Well, so far, for me, this is kind of a Gentlemen's war:
6:30am my houseboy (tentboy!), Kim, awakens me
And pours hot water for shaving
Hot water! My God! In a war!
And a boy!
All hands have boys, even troops on the line
They do all the work — KP, carrying, etc.
We sit down to breakfast (in a tent) with
Tablecloth and china plates
No mess kit!
And electric lights!
We sleep on air mattresses
With lots of blankets
Had to leave all my gear behind
In Japan
If you send things, don't send large packages
Shoebox size — but please send often!
I hear tell there isn't a piano in the whole of Korea!
Maybe I'll get to one in Japan at Christmas
I'll call you then — we'll cry together
Feel mostly like crying- haven't broken down yet
There is a full moon on the 15th — perhaps I'll cry then
All my kisses for you and our children.
Tomorrow is Little Glory's 5th birthday.
Too bad I didn't get to do anything for her.
Did you for me,
Oh, my Gloria?

101

Dark Vegetable Stock*

Use this stock when a deep color and strong, smoky flavors will enhance the recipe, like a vegetarian version of French Onion Soup.
It can be kept for up to 5 days in the refrigerator, or frozen for up to 2 months.

2 yellow onions, unpeeled, quartered
6 shallots
8 cloves garlic, unpeeled
1 carrot, washed,
brushed and cut in half
six stalks celery, cut in half
2 each parsnips, turnips, rutabagas,
washed, brushed and cut in half
5-6 quarts water
salt and pepper
lemongrass stalk

Preheat an oven to 400°. Spread the vegetables on a baking sheet. Toss lightly with olive oil salt and pepper. Place in the oven and roast, turning the vegetables at least once during cooking, until the vegetables are well darkened on some surfaces, about 55 minutes. (Parchment can be used to preserve the pan).

Transfer the vegetables to a large stock pot and fill with water. Bring barely to a boil, then reduce the heat to low and simmer uncovered without allowing the water to bubble, for about 3 hours. Don't ever boil any stock — the protein particles will start to separate and fall apart and make the stock cloudy. The stock should be deeply colored and very aromatic. Add more water if necessary.

Strain through a fine-mesh sieve into containers. Let cool. Cap tightly, and refrigerate or freeze.

*This recipe can become robust chicken stock by adding roasted bones with the other ingredients.

Glory's 5th Birthday

Junior and I sprinkled the Big House kitchen table with confetti — discarded paper doll clothes and magazine pictures we had industriously cut into tiny bits with our little girl scissors. Martin and Little Jon sat near-by, blowing up purple balloons, on which Gloria tied long purple ribbons. She hung the balloons from the ceiling over the table, creating a canopy of floating purple balls, drifting above us.

Flossie fried chicken, sending one of my favorite aromas wafting our way, while Bessie mashed potatoes. A **Boston Cream Pie** sat in the refrigerator, awaiting its presentation.

Gloria sent the four cousins scurrying upstairs to Junior and Little Jon's attic room, where our party clothes awaited us, tenderly laid out across the beds. I scrambled into my silky blouse and brown taffeta jumper, changing my shoes and socks from sneakers and cotton to Mary Janes and lace. Speed demons, we dressed and flew back down the stairs.

Our party guests were arriving: Pop and Marnie, attired, in my honor to the nines, in dark suit and purple silken lace, respectively; Big Jon and Aunt T; Slick, of course; Lincoln; Flossie (in purple turban!); Bessie; and Mr. Talbot. With the whole Farm crew, there were enough Folks to spill out the door, or to use the formal dining room, but still I wanted my party in the Kitchen, at the oak table, my symbol of Home. Somehow, when it came time to sit, we squeezed together, chairs clacking, skirts rustling, elbows rubbing. These were my people, minus one father, and this was my birthday.

Martin sang to me, a cappella, "Today is a Birthday," the Big Jon & Sparkie song we both knew by heart, being major fans of their radio show "No School Today." Martin and I sang that song to everyone we could think of for several years, even if it wasn't their birthday.

Sparkie: a little elf from the land of make-believe, who "thought like a regular boy." Right down my alley. Big Jon, not my uncle, but the voice on the radio, was Sparkie's daddy figure. The opening theme of the show was Teddy Bears' Picnic, a song that *my* Daddy (where was he again?) played for me on the piano.

Today is a Birthday

"Today is a birthday
We wonder for whom
We know it is someone
Who's right in this room

So, look all around you
For somebody who
Is smiling and happy
My goodness it's you!

Happy birthday, Glory,
From all of us to you
Happy birthday, Glory
From Mommy and Daddy, too

We congratulate you
And pray good luck follows you
Happy Birthday, Glory
May all of your dreams come true!"

Boston Cream Pie

The Pastry Cream

4 eggs
Pinch of salt
3/4 cup granulated sugar
3 tablespoons cake flour
4 tablespoons cornstarch
3 1/3 cups hot whole milk
3 tablespoons unsalted butter,
cut in pieces
2 teaspoons vanilla

Beat the eggs with the salt until slightly thickened, about 2 minutes on high speed. Gradually beat in the sugar on medium speed. When all the sugar has been added, increase the speed to high, and beat until the mixture is thick and pale, forming a ribbon when the beater is raised. Add the cake flour and cornstarch and beat them in on low speed until incorporated. Scrape the bowl. While beating on very low speed, gradually add the hot milk. Transfer the mixture to a 4- to 5-quart saucepan and cook over medium heat, stirring almost constantly with a heatproof rubber spatula. If the mixture becomes lumpy, switch begin whisking constantly, until the mixture is very thick. Bring to a boil. Cook an additional 2 to 3 minutes, whisking. Remove the pan from heat and whisk in the butter and vanilla. Scrape the pastry cream into a bowl and spread a bit of butter across its surface. Cool and refrigerate overnight.

The Cake

2 cups sifted cake flour
1 1/2 teaspoons baking powder
1/4 teaspoon salt
1/2 cup (1 stick) unsalted butter
1 cup granulated sugar
1 teaspoon vanilla extract
3 eggs
1 egg yolk
2/3 cup whole milk

Adjust an oven rack to the center position and preheat the oven to 325°. Butter a 10-inch round cake pan, line the bottom with a round of parchment, and butter the paper. Dust the bottom of the pan only with all-purpose flour, and whack out the excess. Set the pan aside. Resift the flour with the baking powder and salt 3 times; set aside. Beat the butter with an electric mixer until smooth and creamy. On medium speed, beat the sugar in 1/4 cup at a time, beating between additions. When all the sugar has been absorbed, beat on medium speed for 4 to 5 minutes. Scrape the bowl and beat in the vanilla. Add the eggs one at a time, beating on medium-high speed about 30 seconds after each. Add the yolk and beat 1 minute more. Scrape the bowl and beater as necessary. On lowest speed, add the flour alternately with the milk, beginning and ending with the dry ingredients. Beat only until each addition is thoroughly incorporated. Scrape the batter into the prepared cake pan. The batter will level, and some of it will move up the side of the pan, leaving the center a bit lower. This is as it should be. Bake 35 to 45 minutes, until the cake is pale golden brown and springs back when gently pressed in the center. Cool the cake in its pan on a wire rack for 10 minutes. Unmold the cake onto a cooling rack. Remove the pan and paper, cover the cake with another cooling rack, and invert to cool right side up. Cool completely before using.

The Chocolate Ganache

1/3 cup whipping cream
7 ounces semisweet or bittersweet chocolate, chopped

Bring the whipping cream to a boil in a small, heavy saucepan. Remove the pan from the heat and immediately add the chocolate. Stir with a whisk until the chocolate is melted and the mixture is completely smooth. Use while warm.

To Assemble

Level the cake with a serrated knife. Cut the cake layer in half horizontally. Place a dab of pastry cream in the center of a cardboard circle to hold the cake in place, and set the bottom half of the cake layer, cut side up, on the cardboard. Whisk the chilled pastry cream briefly to smooth it, and spread a thick layer on the cake. The pastry cream should be about 3/4 inch thick. Save the leftover cream.

Set the remaining cake layer on top of the pastry cream. Using a narrow metal spatula, spread a thin layer of pastry cream around the side of the cake. Save any remaining pastry cream for another use.

Set the cake on a dessert platter. If you make four strips of parchment, laying them in a square around the platter before placing the cake, you can preserve the platter from drops of ganache while you frost the cake. Whisk the warm **Chocolate Ganache** to smoothness and pour it onto the center of the cake. Spread it evenly with a narrow metal spatula right to the edge of the cake, letting just a drizzle of it run down the side. After it is cooled, remove the parchment carefully from the platter.

Refrigerate at least 1 to 2 hours. Cut while still cold, but wait about fifteen minutes to let it come to room temperature before serving, if you can wait that long.

Serves 12.

James
Oct 1ˢᵗ, 1951
My Own,
Nighttime
Time to miss you keenly again
Missing is more intense with memories
Popping up here and there
Unannounced
Breaking into my turbulent thoughts
Little things like **Daddy's Favorite Garlic Bread.**
I should have stayed a corporal
And Leader of the Band
I might still be there, with you
But I had to come, my Gloria
Looks like everyone will have to come
The Peace talks *are* resuming, though
Pray God for a peace soon
Please include New Yorker magazines in boxes

Daddy's Favorite Garlic Bread

Make the French Bread recipe in baguette style. When cooled, or with day old bread, slice length-wise through the middle. Lay the bread crust side down on a baking sheet covered with parchment. Lightly toast in a 325° oven. Remove from oven and rub a peeled clove of garlic over toasted bread. The more you rub, the more garlicky your bread. Spread bread with butter and perhaps Parmesan cheese, or Cheddar cheese. Return to oven and bake until golden and bubbly, about five minutes.

Clear Vegetable Stock
Makes 4 quarts

2 carrots, cut in large chunks
3 celery stalks, cut in large chunks
2 large white onions, quartered, skins on
1 head of garlic, halved
1 each rutabaga, parsnip, turnip, halved
2 bay leaves
1 teaspoon salt
4 quarts water

Brush and clean the vegetables and place in a large stockpot over medium heat. Add about 4 quarts water. Toss in the bay leaves and salt and allow it to slowly come to a simmer. Lower the heat to medium-low and gently simmer for 3 hours, partially covered.

Carefully strain the stock through a fine sieve into another pot to remove the vegetable solids. Use the stock immediately or if you plan on storing it, place the pot in a sink full of ice water and stir to cool down the stock. Cover and refrigerate for up to one week or freeze.

James

Oct 5th, 1951

Now a month since we last talked

Makes for blue notes

No happy tunes in my head

Clear Chicken Stock

1 chicken, plucked and washed

2 carrots, cut in large chunks

3 celery stalks, cut in large chunks

2 large white onions, quartered

1 head of garlic, halved

1 each: rutabaga, parsnip, turnip, halved

2 bay leaves

1 teaspoon salt

3 quarts water

Brush and clean the vegetables and place in a large stockpot over medium heat. Add about 3 quarts water. Gently place whole chicken in the pot. Toss in the bay leaves and salt and allow it to slowly come to a simmer. Lower the heat to medium-low and gently simmer for 3 hours, partially covered.

Carefully strain the stock through a fine sieve into another pot to remove the vegetable solids. Use the stock immediately or if you plan on storing it, place the pot in a sink full of ice water and stir to cool down the stock. Cover and refrigerate for up to one week or freeze.

Gloria
Oct 9th, 1951
Cable:

From the Farm to Yokohama:

Family well but lonely. Letters mailed. Love Gloria

Dark Chicken Stock

1 chicken, cut in pieces

2 carrots, cut in large chunks

3 celery stalks, cut in large chunks

2 large white onions, quartered

1 head of garlic, halved

1 each rutabaga, parsnip, turnip, halved

Dried herbs

2 bay leaves

1 teaspoon salt

3 quarts water

Cover two baking trays with parchment. Place chicken pieces on one, the vegetables on the other. Coat with olive oil, salt and herbs. Roast in 350° oven for about an hour. Remove from oven and cool to a handling point. Place roasted chicken pieces and vegetables in a large stockpot over medium heat. Add about 3 quarts water. Toss in the bay leaves and salt and allow it to slowly come to a simmer. Lower the heat to medium-low and gently simmer for 3 hours, partially covered. Be careful not to boil the stock. This causes the protein bits to separate and cloud an otherwise beautiful stock. Remove from heat and cool slightly before the next step.

Carefully strain the stock through a fine sieve into another pot to remove the solids. Use the stock immediately or if you plan on storing it, place the pot in a sink full of ice water and stir to cool down the stock. Cover and refrigerate for up to one week or freeze.

James

Oct 10th, 1951

Thank you for cable — was worried, no letters

So considerate — thoughtful of you

I love you my dearest and await your letters

With new-bridegroom nervousness

Until then, I am nothing but your old lonesome,

Me

Dark Beef Stock

2 pounds beef bones

2 carrots, cut in large chunks

3 celery stalks, cut in large chunks

2 large white onions, quartered

1 head of garlic, halved

1 each rutabaga, parsnip, turnip, halved

2 bay leaves

1 teaspoon salt

3 quarts water

Cover two baking trays with parchment. Place bones on one, the vegetables on the other. Coat with olive oil, salt and herbs. Roast in 350° oven for about an hour. Remove from oven and cool to a handling point. Place roasted beef and vegetables in a large stockpot over medium heat. Add about 3 quarts water. Toss in the bay leaves and salt and allow it to slowly come to a simmer. Lower the heat to medium-low and gently simmer for 3 hours, partially covered. Be careful not to boil the stock. This causes the protein bits to separate and cloud an otherwise beautiful stock. Remove from heat and cool slightly before the next step.

Carefully strain the stock through a fine sieve into another pot to remove the solids. Use the stock immediately or if you plan on storing it, place the pot in a sink full of ice water and stir to cool down the stock. Cover and refrigerate for up to one week or freeze.

Salad

Magic Salads were Gloria's nutritional balance to the Farm's *high protein, lots o' carbohydrates diet* designed for the fast-moving, calorie-burning, hard-laboring staff.

Ohio's growing season is a bit unpredictable, depending upon how harsh or protracted the winter. If we were lucky, Lincoln could start his babies in March in the "green-box," a cool little device he constructed out of nailed-together boards filled with dirt with a couple of old glass windows for lids. If the groundhog predicted a longer winter, he waited until April.

Lincoln provided Gloria several kinds of lettuce and baskets spilling over with bounty — squash, beans, tomatoes, cukes, kohlrabi, broccoli, cabbage, peppers, pumpkins. The cold dirt floor in the Big House basement provided good "wintering-over" for the root vegetables and hardier things, and Gloria's personal goal to get through the winter without purchasing vegetables, except for lettuce.

Fruit Cream a la Gloria
The Fruit:
2 cups fresh seedless grapes, cut in half
4 cups melon balls, cantaloupe or honeydew
4 cups nectarines or peaches, peeled & sliced
2 cups fresh blueberries
2 cups fresh strawberries
2 cups fresh pineapple chunks
1 cup sliced kiwi fruit
Or, you know, whatever!
Combine all fruits and chill.

Serve with:
Fruit Cream
1 8 ounce package cream cheese, softened
1 cup powdered sugar
1 cup whipping cream
Juice from 1 lemon
orange juice
Soften cream cheese, whip with powdered sugar. In a separate bowl, whip cream until it forms soft peaks.

Combine beaten cream cheese, whipped cream, and lemon juice; continue to beat, adding just enough orange juice to achieve a good pouring consistency.

James
Oct 13ᵗʰ, 1951

Remembering our trip across the country
Enclosed is a letter for Little Glory
Dear Little Glory,
I sent Martin some Korean money
and here is some for you, too.
A bit late, but for your birthday.
Maybe you would like to show it
To your friends at school.
Are you having fun at school?
Will you and Martin
build a snowman?
Are you and Herman friends now?
I'll bet you've had fun with the Hay Harvesting!
I see you got to ride the tractor.
Maybe Martin and Momma
will help you write a letter to Daddy.
Love, Daddy

Cucumber Salad

1 medium cucumber, peeled and thinly sliced

1 medium sweet red onion, thinly sliced

2 teaspoons salt

2 Tablespoons sugar

2 Tablespoons vinegar

1 cup cold water

1/4 teaspoon pepper

Mix all ingredients together and chill before serving.

Waldorf Salad

*Oscar Michel Tschirky (1866-1950), maitre d'hôtel at New York's Waldorf Astoria, gets the credit for creating the **Waldorf Salad** for a big society event upon the opening of the new hotel in 1896. He was known as "Oscar of the Waldorf" and worked there almost 50 years! He was a bit of a star - a fixture. Someone other than Oscar added the nuts. Gloria added raisins.*

1 cup granny smith apples, chopped

1 Tablespoon lemon juice

1 cup celery, chopped

1/4 cup mayonnaise

1/4 cup raisins

1/4 cup pecans

Warm German Potato Salad

This is my Uncle Jon's mother's, mother's, mother's recipe, or something like that.

1 pound lean bacon of good quality

2 medium onions, chopped

3/4 cup sugar

1 Tablespoon salt

2 teaspoons celery seed

1/2 teaspoon pepper

1 cup vinegar

1/2 cup water

12 cups thin skinned white potatoes, cooked and diced

parsley

Cook bacon until crisp; drain (reserving 1/4 cup fat), and crumble.

Cook onion in fat until just tender. Blend in sugar, salt, celery seed, and pepper to taste. Add vinegar and water. Cook and stir until thickened and bubbly. Add bacon and potatoes; heat thoroughly, tossing lightly so as not to break up the potato slices.

Garnish with parsley. Serve warm.

Ambrosia Fruit Salad

Ambrosia: food of the gods, delivered by doves. In ancient Greek mythology, only the gods were permitted to eat Ambrosia. I'm not sure they had marshmallows. Some thought that eating Ambrosia would confer immortality upon them, others believed a mortal would disintegrate on the spot if it touched his lips. Gloria just thought it a good way to feed her children fruit.

2 cups fresh mandarin oranges
or 2 cans mandarin oranges, drained
2 cups fresh pineapple chunks
or 2 cans crushed pineapple, drained
1 cup fresh, pitted cherries
1 cup whipped cream
2 cups shredded coconut
2 cups miniature marshmallows

Toss and chill before serving.

Personally, these days I leave out the marshmallows.

Baby Spinach Salad

1 tablespoon butter
3/4 cup almonds, blanched and slivered
1 pound baby spinach, rinsed and dried

Dressing:

2 tablespoons toasted sesame seeds
1 tablespoon poppy seeds
1/2 cup white sugar
2 teaspoons minced onion
2 teaspoons dry mustard
1/4 cup white wine vinegar
1/4 cup cider vinegar
1/2 cup vegetable oil

In a medium saucepan, melt butter over medium heat. Cook and stir almonds in butter until lightly toasted. Remove from heat, and let cool.

In a large bowl, combine the spinach with the toasted almonds.

In a medium bowl, whisk together the sesame seeds, poppy seeds, sugar, onion, dry mustard, white wine vinegar, cider vinegar, and vegetable oil. Toss with spinach just before serving.

Gorgonzola Pear Salad

1/8 cup white sugar
1/2 cup pecans

1 head leaf lettuce, shredded into bite size pieces
3 pears — peeled (optional), cored and chopped into bite size pieces
5 ounces Gorgonzola cheese, crumbled
1/2 cup green onions, thinly sliced

Dressing:

1/3 cup olive oil
3 tablespoons red wine vinegar
1 1/2 teaspoons white sugar
1 1/2 teaspoons prepared mustard
1 clove garlic, chopped
1/2 teaspoon salt
fresh ground black pepper to taste

In a skillet over medium heat, stir 1/4 cup of sugar together with the pecans. Continue stirring gently until sugar has melted and caramelized the pecans. Carefully transfer nuts onto waxed paper. Allow to cool, and break into pieces.

For the dressing, blend oil, vinegar, sugar, mustard, chopped garlic, salt, and pepper.

In a large serving bowl, layer lettuce, pears, Gorgonzola and green onions. Pour dressing over salad, sprinkle with pecans, and serve.

BLT Salad on Pizza

1/2 pound bacon
1/2 cup mayonnaise
2 tablespoons apple cider vinegar
1/4 cup finely chopped fresh basil
4 slices French bread, cut into 1/2 inch pieces

1 teaspoon salt
1 teaspoon ground black pepper
1 tablespoon canola oil
1 pound romaine lettuce - rinsed, dried, and cut into shreds
1 pint cherry tomatoes, halved or two Roma tomatoes, chopped and drained
1 recipe pizza dough*

Place bacon in a large, deep skillet. Cook over medium high heat until evenly brown. Drain, cool, crumble and set aside. Reserve 2 tablespoons of the fat.

In a small bowl, whisk together the reserved bacon fat, mayonnaise, vinegar and basil, cover and let dressing stand at room temperature.

In a large skillet over medium heat, toss the bread pieces with the salt and pepper. Drizzle with the oil, continue tossing and cook over medium-low heat until golden brown.

In a large bowl mix together the romaine, tomatoes, bacon and croutons. Pour the dressing over the salad and toss well.

If making a pizza, roll out dough into 4 individual pizzas and sprinkle with olive oil and salt and pepper and bake until golden but not crisp. Serve salad on individual pizzas which can be rolled up like a wrap.

Pizza Dough

1 cup lukewarm water
1 package active dry yeast
1 tablespoon sugar
2 1/2 - 3 cups flour
2 tablespoons olive oil
1/2 teaspoon salt

Combine the water, yeast and sugar in a bowl. Let stand ten minutes. Add half the flour and stir well. Add the salt and the oil and enough of the remaining flour to form smooth, soft dough. Turn out onto lightly floured board and knead five minutes. If the dough is too sticky, sprinkle with more flour while kneading. Place dough in a lightly oiled bowl and let stand, covered, about 45 minutes. After the dough has risen, place on a lightly floured surface and divide into four pieces. Let stand, covered, 20 minutes. Roll out mini pizzas and bake for BLT Salad on Pizza, or top with sauce, fresh mozzarella cheese and other things of choice. Bake in 375° oven for about 20 minutes.

James
Oct 16th, 1951

Wow! A jackpot of letters today!
Wonderful!
You are concerned about my comfort.
I am well off, considering:
Hot water,
A houseboy to do my washing,
And make my bunk.
I have all sorts of heavy clothes,
Including long-johns not needed yet.
I could use a bed warmer about 5 foot 2,
Eyes of Blue.

I am close *enough* to the shooting
Let's put it that way
No, it is not really dangerous
The Reds do not fly air missions over us
And we are definitely out of artillery range
The "front" from me at this time
Is about as far as from the Farm to Martin's school
I am not trying to minimize the facts

Mixed Greens with Warm Gorgonzola Dressing

4 slices cooked bacon

3/4 cup olive oil

1/3 cup red wine vinegar

1/4 cup sugar

1 teaspoon salt

1 clove garlic, minced

2 ounces crumbled Gorgonzola cheese

6 cups mixed salad greens

2 tablespoons toasted sliced almonds

Combine the olive oil, red wine vinegar, white sugar, salt, garlic, and Gorgonzola cheese in a blender; blend until smooth. Pour the dressing into a small saucepan over medium-low heat and warm gently.

Toss the mixed greens, almonds, and crumbled bacon together in a salad bowl; drizzle dressing over salad and toss to coat. Serve immediately.

James, continued
Your Letters
You are concerned about telling me
The tear-jerking things,
And I must be confess
I choked up at reading about Martin crying —
And the things that he and Little Glory say
But those are exactly the things
I want to hear.
I have discovered how I live for details
All these little things
That you have told me in these letters
Are exactly the things
I have been starved for
Tell all. Spare me nothing.

Christmas
Since you asked,
Send my favorite food stuffs.
I believe I mentioned smoked oysters.
Also, cheese
Bottles and glass inadvisable

French Onion Soup

Oven-proof ramekins
2 lb medium yellow or red onions, thinly sliced
3 sprigs fresh thyme
2 bay leaves
3/4 teaspoon salt
1/2 stick (1/4 cup) unsalted butter
2 teaspoons flour

3/4 cup dry white wine
4 cups beef stock (page 118)
1 1/2 cups water
1/2 teaspoon black pepper
6 (1/2-inch-thick) pieces French Bread
1/2 lb piece Gruyère, sliced thin or shaved
2 tablespoons grated Parmigiano-Reggiano

Cook onions, thyme, bay leaves, and salt in butter in a 4- to 5-quart pot over moderate heat, uncovered, stirring frequently, until onions are very soft and deep golden brown, about 45 minutes.

Add flour and cook, stirring, 1 minute. Stir in wine and cook, stirring, 2 minutes. Stir in stock, water, and pepper and simmer, uncovered, stirring occasionally, 30 minutes.

Preheat oven to 350°F Place a piece of parchment on a baking sheet. Arrange bread in 1 layer on a large and toast, turning over once, until completely dry, about 15 minutes. Do not burn or even make it so hard it might break teeth. Just dry. Remove toast from oven and preheat broiler. Put crocks in a shallow baking pan.

Discard bay leaves and thyme from soup and divide soup among crocks, then float a piece of toast in each. Lay sheets of Gruyère over toast, cover tops of crocks, allowing ends of cheese to hang over rims of crocks, then sprinkle with Parmigiano-Reggiano. Broil 4 to 5 inches from heat until cheese is melted and bubbly, 1 to 2 minutes.

Mandarin Orange Salad

8 cups baby spinach leaves, washed and patted dry

1/2 medium red onion, very thinly sliced and separated into rings

1 fresh, sectioned or

1 (11 ounce) can mandarin oranges, drained, reserve juice*

1 1/2 cups dried cranberries

1 cup toasted sliced almonds

1 cup crumbled feta or dry goat cheese

Balsamic Vinaigrette:
2 teaspoons minced onion
1/4 cup Balsamic vinegar
2 tablespoons brown sugar
1 tablespoon Dijon Mustard
1 large garlic clove, crushed or pressed
1/2 cup olive oil
1/4 cup canola or safflower oil
*if using canned Mandarins, add a little juice to this dressing for flavor

Toss gently and serve.

James, continued
Health

Mine is very good.
So sorry all kids sick with flu, measles
Martin especially, poor little tyke
Give him soup
I wonder if you have any idea…
I want to bring you breakfast in bed,
To rub your back-
To show you off at places —
To drink coffee and eat **Coffee Cake** with you —
And talk with you.
I won't even get into our intimate life —
At this point I dare not even think about it.
Suffice it to say that I love you
And the thought of you-
And the thought of having been with you —
And the thought of again being with you…

I have no fear about the future with you —
And there is no future without you
I give thanks for the rainy night we met —
And remember it with clarity
And I even give thanks for the sadness of our last night —
For it was with you that I shared it

Enough. I can't stand myself

Gloria's Real Coffee Cake
Preheat oven to 325°

1/2 cup butter
1/2 cup sugar
1/2 cup molasses
1 egg
Pinch salt
1 cup flour, approximately
1 teaspoon soda, dissolved in
1 cup strong coffee, cooled

Mix ingredients. Pour into 8 x 8 inch pan. Bake 25-35 minutes, or until knife comes out clean.

Crumb Topping for Muffins and Pies on page 192 can be sprinkled on top before baking, if desired

Halloween

In pink tights, tutu and white wings, wearing tiny white satin ballet shoes on her 5 year old feet, Tinkerbell emerged from the Woodie onto the gravel driveway at Doolittle Meadows, tightly holding in her two hands a long silver star wand, with sparkly ribbons dangling from the top. Her brown eyes were wide with wonder, looking at the bright lights and the open, welcoming front door. Tinkerbell's guardian, 5 foot 2, eyes of blue, scrunched her high heels into the gravel as she walked close behind, with two covered trays of warm **Glazed Donuts**. Behind the guardian sauntered a mini-cowboy, black jeans rolled up at the cuff, black felt hat stitched in white around the edges swinging by a string at his back, cap-gun drawn to protect his womenfolk. The Bakers, minus one, are going to a party. Actually, three parties, but the night is young.

Glazed Donuts

2 packets active dry yeast

1/4 cup lukewarm water

1 1/2 cups lukewarm milk

1/2 cup white sugar

1 teaspoon salt

2 eggs

1/3 butter, softened

5 cups all-purpose flour

1 quart vegetable oil for frying

1/3 cup butter

2 cups powdered sugar

1 1/2 teaspoons vanilla

4 tablespoons hot water or as needed

Sprinkle the yeast into the warm water, and let stand for 5 minutes, or until foamy. In a large bowl, mix together the yeast mixture, milk, sugar, salt, eggs, butter, and 2 cups of the flour. Mix for a few minutes with a wooden spoon, making a "sponge". Let stand five minutes. Beat in remaining flour 1/2 cup at a time, until the dough no longer sticks to the bowl. Knead for about 5 minutes, or until smooth and elastic. Place the dough into a greased bowl, cover and set in a warm place to rise until double.

Turn the dough out onto a floured surface, and roll out to 1/2 inch thickness. Cut with a floured donut cutter. Let donuts sit out to rise again until double. Cover loosely with a cloth.

Melt butter in a saucepan over medium heat. Blend in powdered sugar and vanilla until smooth. Remove from heat, and stir in hot water one tablespoon at a time until the icing is thin, but not watery. Set aside.

Heat the oil in a deep-fryer or large heavy skillet to 350º. Slip donuts into the hot oil using a wide spatula. Turn donuts over as they rise to the surface. Fry donuts on each side until golden brown. Remove from hot oil, to drain on a wire rack. Dip donuts into the glaze while still hot, and set onto wire racks to drain off excess. Keep a cookie sheet or tray under racks for easier clean up.

Martin and I were new to Halloween in the country. No "Knock-knock, Ding-dong, Trick-or-Treat" door-to-door. Farm-by-Farm, it was a progressive family costume party, a movable feast of treating, and just a few tricks.

At the Doolittle's, an abundant fall apple crop was pressed for cider, fermented in casks a few months earlier for the grownups. A long table spread with country food — potato salad, ham, rolls, cheeses, greens - bespoke a good harvest at the Doolittle's.

At the end of a long white string hanging from the rafter in the kitchen dangled a little red apple, at Tinkerbell's eye level. Amongst much laughter and grown-up cheer, someone tied Tink's hands behind her back. She didn't like this much, but Tinkerbell was a patient girl. When Gloria said "Try to catch the apple in your mouth, HoneyBaby, without touching it with your hands," Tinkerbell pondered this for a long moment, looked soulfully up at her cowboy pal in the dashing black boots, and said, "You do it." And so he did.

We bobbed for apples.

We ate **Caramel Apples** and **Polish Apple Dumplings**.

We munched dried apples.

We learned about cider made with bittersweet and bittersharp apples.

45 minutes later, Gloria left her trays of **Glazed Donuts** and took a crate of apples, promising a pie.

Caramel Apples

6 apples of choice

(We prefer sweet apples, like Gala or Fuji, but some like tart Granny Smiths)

1 (14 ounce) package individually wrapped caramels, unwrapped

2 tablespoons milk

Chopped nuts, optional

Remove the stem from each apple and press a craft stick into the top. Lay a piece of parchment on a baking sheet.

Place caramels and milk in the top of a double boiler and simmer over water, stirring once or twice. Allow to cool briefly.

Roll each apple quickly in caramel sauce until well coated. Dip in chopped nuts, if desired. Place on prepared sheet to set.

James
October 20th, 1951

I send you love
On a 45!
Please play enclosed
on the portable record player
When you are putting the children to bed

On to the Littlefields, where the double front doors were obscured by a hay bale tunnel, through which the threesome walked, encumbered with items, same as before. It was only dark for a minute, inside the tunnel, before they emerged into a room filled with Littlefields, little and big: the small ones played Pin the Tail on the Donkey; the medium ones draped their bodies over the furniture, drinking Cokes; the big ones performed a song called, "What would you like to drink, Gloria?" There are a lot of Littlefields and they love a party. That's what Gloria says.

By the time we get to Cobb's Corner to sit for dinner in front of the fire, the donuts meant for Harmon are cold. Tink and the Cowboy are appled-out, up-to-here with donuts, and tired. Gloria, faithful guide through the labyrinth of miniature clowns, pirates, elves, cowboys and Tinkerbells, *and* going to parties in the 'Hood without her hubby, is happy for a respite. We fall asleep on the hearthrug, star wand and black hat on the floor beside us. Gloria enjoys dinner with Harmon, his sister, Doris, and Ralph Washmore, her husband, in flannel shirt and jeans, with an exquisite comb-over, who hardly ever says a word because of an outrageous stutter about which he is monumentally embarrassed. He communicates with Doris in a mix of elaborate gestures and body language only she can decipher. We love Ralph. We think he's so amazingly uncomplicated, because he never talks. Imagine all the unspoken words and the maze of musings inside Ralph.

As we leave, Ralph gestures toward the side table so we'll take home jars of marmalade, bundles of dried corn, pumpkins and **Peanut Butter Cookies**. Gloria leaves the cold but still appreciated donuts and a **Ginger Cake**.

Peanut Butter Cookies

2/3 cup peanut butter
1 egg
1/2 cup butter, softened
1/2 cup brown sugar
1/2 cup sugar
1 teaspoon soda
1/4 teaspoon salt
1 teaspoon vanilla
1 1/2 cups flour

Blend peanut butter, egg and softened butter in mixer. Add dry ingredients. Shape dough into balls. Place on cookie sheet. Flatten with fork. Crisscross.

Bake 10 minutes at 325°.

Ginger Cake

World's most tender, aromatic and delicious ginger cake!

325°
6 oz. butter, softened
3/4 cup brown sugar
4 egg yolks
1 cup dark molasses
2" piece fresh ginger, grated
1 cup crystallized ginger, chopped
1/3 cup yogurt
2 cups flour
1/2 teaspoon nutmeg
1/2 teaspoon ground cloves
1/2 teaspoon ground cinnamon
1/2 teaspoon ground ginger

1 tablespoon baking soda in 1 tablespoon hot water
4 egg whites

Cream butter and sugar well. Add yolks one at a time. Add molasses, fresh ginger, crystallized ginger and yogurt. Blend well. Transfer to a large bowl and sift in dry ingredients. Best egg whites until stiff. While you're beating the egg whites, activate baking soda in hot water. Add this to batter. Gently fold beaten egg whites into batter 1/3 at a time. Pour into well sprayed 9x12 inch pan (or a Bundt Pan), spreading batter evenly across. Bake at 325° for approximately 40 minutes. Serve warm (with whipped cream!)

Polish Apple Dumplings with Sherry Sauce

6 Granny Smith apples, peeled and cored
6 Lemon Pastry Squares, recipe below
1/2 cup brown sugar
1/2 teaspoon cinnamon
3 tablespoons butter
1 cup sweet sherry
1/2 cup water
1/2 cup sugar

Place each apple on a pastry square. Mix sugar, cinnamon and butter and spoon into center of apples. Fold up pastry square around apples and moisten with sherry to seal, making little packets. Prick outside of pastry packet with fork. Place about one inch apart on shallow baking pan that has been non-stick sprayed. Bake in 350° oven about 15 minutes, until the pastry begins to turn golden. Meanwhile, place sherry, water and sugar in a saucepan and bring to a boil. Simmer 5 minutes. Pour a little syrup around the apples in the pan. Bake an additional 15 minutes. Serve with remaining syrup and whipped cream.

Lemon Pastry Squares

2 cups sifted all-purpose flour
1 teaspoon salt
3/4 cup butter
1 tablespoon lemon juice
3 or 4 tablespoons cold water

Place dry ingredients in food processor and blend until mealy. Add lemon juice and cold water while processing — adding enough water to bring the dough together. Roll in flour and set aside for ten minutes. Roll into six squares.

Gloria
November 1, 1951
My Own, Dear Lovely One,
I cannot speak from sobbing, I cannot write from the tears.
Your voice, your own sweet, resonant voice. How did you
ever think of doing that, recording yourself reading Martin and
Glory's favorite story? Martin cried to hear your voice, Glory
a bit puzzled — started looking for you in the closet, under
the bed, like you were hiding. She didn't quite understand
when I told her it was a recording, but settled into the story,
nonetheless.

ME

The Little Red Hen

As read by James to his children from 5,000 miles away

Once upon a time, there was a little red hen who lived on a farm. She was friends with a lazy dog, a sleepy cat, and a noisy yellow duck.

One day the little red hen found some wheat seeds on the ground. The little red hen had an idea. She would plant the wheat.

The little red hen asked her friends, "Who will help me plant the wheat?"

"Not I," barked the lazy dog.

"Not I," purred the sleepy cat.

"Not I," quacked the noisy yellow duck.

"Then I'll do it myself," said the little red hen. And she did.

When the seeds had grown, the little red hen asked her friends, "Who will help me harvest the wheat?"

"Not I," barked the lazy dog.

"Not I," purred the sleepy cat.

"Not I," quacked the noisy yellow duck.

"Then I'll do it myself," said the little red hen. And so she did.

When all the wheat was harvested, the little red hen asked her friends, "Who will help me take the wheat to the mill and grind it into flour?"

"Not I," barked the lazy dog.

"Not I," purred the sleepy cat.

"Not I," quacked the noisy yellow duck.

"Then I'll do it myself," sighed the little red hen. So the little red hen brought the wheat to the mill all by herself, ground the wheat into flour, all by herself, and carried the heavy sack of flour back to the farm. All by…herself.

The tired little red hen asked her friends, "Who will help me bake the bread?"
"Not I," barked the lazy dog.
"Not I," purred the sleepy cat.
"Not I," quacked the noisy yellow duck.

"Then I will," said the little red hen. So the little red hen baked the bread all by herself.

When the bread was finished, the tired little red hen asked her friends, "Who will help me eat the bread?"

"I will!" barked the lazy dog.
"I will!" purred the sleepy cat.
"I will!" quacked the noisy yellow duck.

"No!" said the little red hen. "I will eat the bread all by myself. And so she did."

James
Nov 1, 1951

My Own Darling,
Tonight I kind of feel like talking to you —
And I hope to Jesus I am not interrupted
About a million times
God willing,
I shall devote the next moments
Only to my precious little wife

Oh for just a few minutes
To sit down and have a talk with you.
However, a few minutes would not do,
For I would want to
Prolong it for hours then days.
When next I sit down with you,
I do not wish it ever to end.

Of course,
My absence from the children is
The second hardest thing for me to bear-
The effect my absence has on *them*,
But I am hoping we can rectify it.
Perhaps I'll make them our **World's Greatest Pancakes**
Will they remember me then?

James
Nov 16ᵗʰ, 1951

Yes, report every incident no matter how sad

I want to know what is going on at home

You *are* keeping me well posted

Kids all sick! Oh!

The 45 of **The Little Red Hen**-

If you play it often,

Will they remember my voice?

Thanksgiving

Aside from pickles, Doris Washmore was a master of recipes and crafts using corn, making it her general occupation to recycle her brother's crop debris, husks *and* cobs. She won ribbons at the County Fair for cornhusk dolls, made in the Kickapoo style.

Doris and Ralph both smoked beautiful cob pipes, hers a more delicate version of his. They crafted in winter, around the same time of day Lincoln worked on his rugs.

Ralph and Doris laid the cobs out on screens in the barn to dry for a couple of years. They hollowed out the cobs to make bowl shapes, dipped them in something-or-other to seal the fibers and varnished them on the outside. Ralph carved, hollowed and stained little pine shanks for stems. Cobb's Cobs!

Doris liked to sit outside the barn door in the winter sun, smoking her pipe in the late afternoons, coat open, stockings rolled down over her knees, skirts hiked up for some air, buckets of husks soaking in warm water at her side. A little rickety card table held her kit: string, scissors, piles of dry husks, corn hair, ribbon, little baskets of braided arms and legs, and some flattened husks she'd colored with food coloring and ink for clothing.

Doris was fond of cherry-flavored tobacco. Her grey hair capped her head with tight little curls. Comfortable, loose house dresses draped over Doris like sacks of grain, her round body covered by voluminous folds of bias-cut cotton prints.

Our Thanksgiving table was filled with handsome decorations, thanks to the four cousins, and Doris: painted gourds, corn husk dolls, multi-colored Indian corn bundles, mini pumpkins, paper doll pilgrims, construction paper turkeys.

Doris brought the **Corn Pudding**.

Doris's Corn Pudding

2 cups fresh corn or

2 cups frozen corn or (don't tell Doris)

2 cans cream style corn

3 eggs, slightly beaten

1 cup half & half

2 tablespoons butter, melted

1 tablespoon grated onion

1 teaspoon sugar

1/8 teaspoon salt

Dash of pepper

Combine corn and eggs. Stir in half & half and melted butter and mix well. Add grated onion, sugar, salt and pepper. Blend well. Pour into sprayed 1 1/2 quart casserole dish. Set in pan of hot water and bake at 325° for 1 hour, or until inserted knife comes out clean.

Gloria's Stuffing/Dressing

One large loaf of bread,
perhaps a lovely egg bread,
but any bread will do, cut into cubes
1 pound good quality organic
sausage meat, ground
1/2 cup (1 stick) butter, cut in pieces
6 stalk(s) celery, chopped
2 carrots, chopped
1 onion, chopped
2 teaspoons salt
1 teaspoon coarsely ground black pepper
1 cup fresh parsley leaves, chopped
1 tablespoon fresh thyme leaves, chopped
1tablespoon fresh sage leaves, chopped
3 1/2 cups chicken or turkey stock
1 1/4 cups mixed dried fruit, chopped
(dates, apricots, cranberries, raisins…)

Preheat oven to 350° F. Divide bread between two baking sheets covered with parchment. Toast bread 15 minutes until golden, rotating pans and stirring once.

Heat 12-inch skillet over medium-high heat. Add sausage and cook 5 to 8 minutes or until sausage is browned, stirring. With slotted spoon, transfer sausage to very large bowl. Discard fat. In same skillet, melt butter over medium heat. Add celery, carrot, onion, salt, and pepper. Cook 20 minutes or until vegetables are soft, stirring occasionally. Stir in parsley, thyme, and sage, and cook 2 minutes longer.

While vegetables are cooking, in 2-quart saucepan, heat broth and dried fruit to boiling over high heat. Remove saucepan from heat.

Add vegetable mixture to bowl with meat, stock and dried fruit, and bread cubes; toss. Will stuff up to a 16-pound turkey or in a greased 13-inch by 9-inch glass baking dish. Cover with foil and bake in 325° oven 30 minutes. Remove cover; bake 15 minutes longer or until heated through and lightly browned on top.

Green Beans a la Flossie Forester

2 pounds lightly steamed green beans
1/2 cup sliced or slivered almonds
2 tablespoons butter
Pinch salt
Grated orange rind or zest

Sauté almonds in butter until golden. Add beans and coat with butter and almonds, and cook about five minutes, until beans are heated through. Toss with zest and serve immediately.

Roasted Maple Sweet Potatoes

6 sweet potatoes, peeled and cut into bite size
1/4 cup olive oil
2 tablespoons melted butter
Salt and pepper
1/4 cup maple syrup

Place sweet potatoes in shallow casserole and toss with olive oil and butter. Salt and pepper to taste. Sprinkle with half the maple syrup. Bake in high oven, 400°, about twenty minutes, or until golden, turning once or twice. Toss with remaining maple syrup, if desired. Serve immediately.

Cranberry Relish
most amazing

1 bag fresh cranberries
1 cup dried cherries
1 cup dried cranberries
1 cup brown sugar (more if you like it sweet)
1/2 cup crystalized ginger, chopped
1/2 cup orange juice

Simmer all ingredients until fresh cranberries begin to pop. Cool and keep in refrigerator until ready to use.

GINNA BB GORDON

The Best Pumpkin Pie

1 cup heavy cream

1 1/2 cups pureed pumpkin

2/3 cup packed light brown sugar

2 large eggs

1 teaspoon ground cinnamon

1/2 teaspoon ground ginger

1/4 teaspoon salt

9" pie or tart pan; pie weights or dried beans
Parchment paper

Make pie shell:

Preheat oven to 350° with rack in middle. Roll out dough into a 15-inch round on a lightly floured surface with a lightly floured rolling pin, fit into pie pan. Trim excess dough, leaving a 1/2-inch overhang. Fold overhang in and press to edge of pan so pastry stands slightly above rim. Chill about 30 minutes, until firm.

Lightly prick bottom of shell all over with a fork, line with parchment and fill with pie weights. Bake tart shell until side is set and edge is pale golden, 25 to 30 minutes. Carefully remove weights and foil and bake shell until bottom and side are golden, about 15 minutes more. Cool completely in pan on a rack, about 30 minutes.

Make filling and bake pie:

Whisk together cream, pumpkin purée, brown sugar, eggs, cinnamon, ginger, and salt until smooth.

158

Put pie shell in pan on a baking sheet.

Bake until filling is set a few inches from edge, still wobbly in center, 50 -60 minutes. Cool in pan on a rack, 1 hour. (Filling will continue to set as it cools.)

Pie is best the day it is baked.

Corn-Spoon

3 eggs, separated
1 1/4 cups milk, scalded
3/4 cup corn meal
3/4 teaspoon salt
2 tablespoons butter
2 cups fresh corn or
2 cups frozen or
(dare I say it)
1 can cream style corn
3/4 teaspoon baking powder

Spray a 2 quart shallow baking dish. Stir cornmeal and salt into scalded milk and cook over low heat for a few seconds until the mixture thickens into mush. Blend in butter and corn. Add eggs and blend in. Cool.

Beat egg whites until stiff. Fold into cooled egg and corn mixture, adding baking powder, and pour into prepared baking dish. Bake in hot (375°) oven for about 35 minutes or until golden and puffy. Serve immediately with spoon.

The Christmas Tree

There isn't much to do right now
And so it seems to me
That now's the time to have a chat
Around the Christmas Tree

So mix a batch of cocktails
Martinis, if you please,
And get on something comfy
And come and be at ease.

We'll sit before the fireplace
And watch the dancing flames
And dream about the fun we've had
And talk about our aims

We'll talk about the trips we've made
Across a dozen states
And laugh again at little things
That happened on our dates

(For every day I've spent with you
A date has been to me
We've had such fun and love, you know,
With sadness and with glee)

We'll talk about our love and how
It's lasted eight good years
And praise the day we met, and laugh
At things that once brought tears

The Glory of it all, I think
Is that we're man and wife
We've stuck together quite a spell
And still we're good for life

Our children are the ones we want
We'll plan their futures for them
(And they, like all the normal kids,
Will, as to plans, ignore them!)

Sing a song of romance
I will play the tune
Love like ours is perfect
At midnight or at noon

Yes, fill the glasses up again
Then snuggle up the closer
We'll dream a dream of things to come
And think not of the grosser

So, light the Christmas Tree, my dear,
And sit before the fire
I'll be there soon as e'er I can
For that is my desire

If I don't make it quite on time
We'll drink a toast the same
"To us" and "to the future," dear
We'll set the world aflame

For tho we're miles and miles apart
The sky will be a-light
The current of our love will shine
Through every bloomin' night

Enough for now, my little love
Thank God He sent you from above.

Christmas

Plans at the Farm began in October, since Pop, on an upswing, loved a good party. Marnie wrote out invitations, hoping...

Gloria, Flossie and Bessie kicked in in early December, filling the kitchen and freezer with cookie dough, bread ingredients, snacks and meat dishes for 100 guests — neighbors, business associates, family and friends, all braving the snow-plowed roads to stand next to our Hearth in the Big Living Room (another velvet-lined place in the house no one used unless Marnie and Pop hosted a party).

In the days getting closer to the event, I washed and dried the cookie cutters fifty million times, standing on my little stool. I dipped tops and bottoms of one billion cut cookie shapes into white sugar, spread them with jam and pressed the two pieces together; I stirred gallons of melting chocolate. Then, the day of the party, I got *out* of Gloria's way.

"Lincoln?" Gloria yelped, seeing the only grown-up person in the room with free hands as she was rather unsuccessfully maneuvering the 25 pound turkey out of the oven and onto a platter. He leapt to her aid, just short of saving the bird from a slippery, floor-plopping disaster.

The two of them stood looking at the distressed bird, half on the platter on the floor. The rest of us paused in our work (I, stringing popcorn for the Christmas tree; Martin sniffling and honking into a tissue while perusing his Boys' Life Magazine; Junior counting toothpicks; Little Jon fidgeting with the doilies spread on the plank table, wracking his little brain for an escape plan to get to all that good sledding snow outside; and Flossie and Bessie up to their armpits in dough) and looked at Gloria and Lincoln looking at *it*. A pause and, with the grace of a gazelle, Lincoln swept the bird and the platter onto the table in front of us. As the cousins jumped back in our seats, he grinned at Gloria, defying her to cry over spilt, uhm, turkey.

Christmas Cookies

Of all the things I could say about Gloria's cooking, the highest of all high compliments would be that she cooked with Love. You could see the Love in her face — she focused right in on the set-up, the ingredients, the process, the packaging. She entered the cookies. She became the cookies. She filled the cookies with a sense of longing, or a smile of remembrance, a thought of happiness. When it came to her Christmas Baskets, no one surpassed the outpouring of Love. The nuns, business acquaintances, friends, and of course the little members of the Sugar-Baker family looked forward every year to **"Gloria's Gloria,"** her baskets of Christmas. Until the final few years of her life, Gloria made baskets full of **"Gloria's Gloria"** and sent them all around the town, the country, and sometimes to foreign countries.

Gloria's Gloria
Spitzbuben

Makes 5 dozen German "Jam Cookies."

Heat oven to 350 °

1 cup granulated sugar

1 cup plus 3 tablespoons soft butter

2 cups ground almonds

1 teaspoon vanilla

3 1/2 cups sifted all-purpose flour

Raspberry Jam

Baker's Superfine granulated sugar

Mix together sugar, soft butter, nuts and vanilla. Mix in flour. Knead dough very well. On a lightly floured, cloth covered board, roll to 1/8 to 1/4 inch thickness. Cut with simple cutters. Place on a parchment- lined cookie sheet. Bake about 20 minutes or until lightly browned. Let cool. Spread half the cookies with jam. Top with matching cookie. Dip in Superfine Sugar. Will keep in airtight container for several weeks. Good holiday keepers.

James
14 Dec, 1951

Used some of the SugarShave you sent
They changed the formula!
Smells like bourbon!
What's the pitch? Kindly explain.

Pastry Queen

Z' French Great Aunt Eleanor braved the kitchen in the Big House during the Christmas holiday to impart her vast knowledge of perfect Pastry Dough. I perched on a high stool at the counter, tracking every good thing from her lips and hands. Words and actions were all — recipe left at home, it was all in her head, anyway.

Flossie and Gloria graciously stepped aside to learn while Aunt Eleanor "cut the butter" into the flour with a knife, then rubbed her fingers together with flour and butter to combine it— the ideal "coarse meal" blend for the flaky pastry of Gloria's dreams. Me, I throw the flour and cut-up pieces of butter into the Food Processor and zip-zip. I use Flossie's trick of listening, though, to hear the moment when to stop adding the cold liquid and when to desist blending the dough. Too much liquid and it is mush, too much blending and it's a rock hard calamity.

Basic Pastry Dough
Makes one two-crust pie or
two pies with a bottom crust and a crumble topping.

2 1/2 cups pastry flour
1 1/2 cups unsalted butter, cut in pieces
1/2 teaspoon salt
1/4 to 1/2 cup orange juice

Blend first four ingredients in food processor until butter is distributed and the mixture looks and feels like coarse meal. Slowly add orange juice through top of food processor until a ball of dough begins to form. Do not add too much juice or the dough will be too sticky. Remove from processor, form into a ball, dust with flour, wrap in plastic and refrigerate for 1 hour or overnight. Roll out onto floured board for pies, pasties or other pastry items.

Lemon Pie Filling
1 1/4 cups sugar
2/3 cup sifted cake flour
1/4 cup cornstarch
pinch of salt
1 1/2 cups water
5 egg yolks
1/2 cup lemon juice
2 tablespoons lemon zest

Place first five ingredients in saucepan. Cook until thickened, about ten minutes. Remove from heat. Add five egg yolks, one at a time. Return to heat. Cook, stirring constantly until thick and smooth. Add lemon juice and zest. Set aside. When cooled completely, pour into baked pie shell. The five leftover egg whites may be turned into a meringue for the top.

Pastry Dough Snacks
Perks during baking time

Cookies

When cutting away the remaining dough around the edges of a pie, set aside on cookie sheets. Spread with soft butter, sprinkle with sugar, cinnamon and a pinch of salt. Bake at 325° for about five minutes.

Kids' Pigs in a Blanket

Wrap extra rolled out pastry dough around a cooked hot dog or sausage and bake it for five minutes.

Turnovers

Fill rolled out pastry dough with several berries sprinkled with sugar and dotted with butter. Roll up and bake about five minutes.

French Apple Pie

400° one 9" pie tin
1/2 recipe Basic Pastry Dough
1 cup Muffin Topping (page 192)
8 granny smith apples, peeled, cored and cut into 1" pieces
1 stick unsalted butter
1/2 cups dark brown sugar
1/2 teaspoon salt
2 tablespoons cornstarch mixed with a few drops of water to form a paste
1/3 cup sour cream

Melt butter and sugar in a large skillet. Add apples and toss to coat with butter and sugar mixture. Simmer for about fifteen minutes, until bubbling. Mix in cornstarch mixture and cook for 30 seconds, until thickened. Pour onto baking sheet to cool. Add sour cream.

Roll out pastry dough onto flour-covered board. Place in pie tin. Form flutes around edges. Fill with apple mixture. Sprinkle with Muffin Topping page 173 and bake about 40 minutes, or until Pastry is light brown.

"Gloria's Gloria"
Exquisite Chocolate Mint Sticks
350°

2 sq. (2 oz.) unsweetened chocolate
1/2 cup butter
2 eggs
1 cup sugar

1/4 teaspoon peppermint extract
1/2 cup sifted all-purpose flour
Dash of salt
1/2 cup chopped un-blanched almonds

Grease or spray a 9 inch square glass cake pan. Melt chocolate and butter over hot water. Beat eggs until frothy and stir in sugar, chocolate mixture, peppermint extract. Add flour, salt and almonds. Mix thoroughly. Pour into pan and bake 20 minutes. Cool. Spread top with a thin layer of this filling:

Filling

2 tablespoons soft butter
1 cup sifted confectioner's sugar
1 tablespoon cream
3/4 teaspoon peppermint extract

Work butter into sugar, cream and peppermint extract. Stir until smooth. Keep filling-covered cake in the refrigerator while you make this simple glaze:

172

Glaze

1 sq. (1 oz.) unsweetened chocolate

1 tablespoon butter

Melt chocolate and butter over hot water. Mix thoroughly and dribble over the cool, firm filling. Tilt cake back and forth until glaze covers surface. Refrigerate for at least five minutes.

Cut into strips 2 1/4 inches long and 3/4 inches wide.

James
17 Dec 1951

You are riled, disgusted, saddened
By the turn of the peace talks
Fifteen days later now,
And the talks are still bogging down.
Frankly, we don't pay much attention —
We can't, you know? …ponder that too much.
And most of us now have dismissed the subject
From general conversation-
We still hope.
You speak strongly of the apathy at home
We are aware of it and of course, deplore it.
Can't ponder that too much, either
It is the waste of blood and toil that rankles

Hope the Chloremycin works for Martin's illness.
If not, the answer must be Arizona.
Maybe we can go there.

"Gloria's Gloria"
French Waffle Sandwiches

Dough:
2 1/2 cups sifted all-purpose flour
1 cup butter
1/3 cup water
1 tablespoon vinegar
1/2 to 3/4 cup sugar
Filling:
1 cup butter, softened
1/2 cup confectioner's sugar
1 egg yolk

Sift flour into a bowl and cut the butter in with a pastry blender (farm method. My method: throw in a food processor and zip-zip) until mixture looks like corn meal. Stir (or pour) in water and vinegar and knead a minute or two. Chill for 20 minutes.

Preheat oven to 450°. Divide dough into two or three portions — keep dough not being worked in refrigerator for easier handing). Roll out dough about 1/8' thick. Cut into round cookies about 1 inch in diameter. Put several tablespoons of sugar on parchment and roll out each cookie into the sugar. Keep to round shape, about two inches. Place cookies, sugar side up, on baking sheet covered with parchment. Bake 8-10 minutes, or until sugar begins to caramelize.

For Filling, cream butter until smooth. Add confectioner's sugar and egg yolk and beat until creamy. Spread a thin layer of filling on the bottom of a cookie, cover with the bottom of another cookie — in other words, sugar side out.

Makes about 50 cute and delicious little Waffle Sandwiches.

Gloria

Dec 21, 1951

Hey you!

*That **is** bourbon! And a $6 bottle of Old Granddad, at that! And you are using it as after-shaving lotion!*

I am surprised at you. I kept giving you hints like SugarShave being good for snake bites, and "Old Granddad was sending you some SugarShave." Guess my little joke backfired.

You were supposed to get two bottles, one was genuine SugarShave. Anyway,

I hope there is some bourbon left to drink!

Had a party for 100 of Dad's nearest and dearest, who all, every last one of them, send you big hellos. The weather is so bad, Dad had to walk the mile up Sugar Lane in snow shoes several days before the party. He had a man bull-doze all day so guests could drive in.

Enclosed is the menu. Hired extra help, thank God, or I would be dead.

*Dad **up**, a little expansive, fortunately did not give away the Farm. Got through the party well. Whew.*

Rain on top of snow, now. Kids home all week for Christmas vacation, but cooped up inside with various coughs and ailments. Zero-blast expected tonight. California — Arizona! Here I come! Whichever!

I am glad you got your boxes. I am now dealing with an excess of bananas from the Market.

G

177

Buffet Party Menu
printed in Bessie's hand

Mushroom Caps

Veggie Trays with French Onion Dip

Cheese Balls

Roasted Turkey

Honey Baked Ham

Potatoes au Gratin

Sweet 'n Sour Red Cabbage

Ambrosia Salad

Bread and Jam

Pumpkin Pie

One Million Assorted Cookies

Sweet n' Sour Cabbage
1 red cabbage, shredded
2 apples, sliced
2 tablespoons butter
2 tablespoons brown sugar
2 tablespoons Balsamic Vinegar
Salt and pepper to taste

Sauté cabbage and apples in butter until soft, about ten minutes. Add remaining ingredients and continue to cook until liquid is absorbed and the cabbage and apples caramelize a bit. Salt and pepper to taste.

"Gloria's Gloria"
Fig Bars

Sift:
1 cup flour
1/2 teaspoon salt
1/8 teaspoon soda

Combine:
1 egg
1/2 cup sugar
1/2 cup molasses
1/4 cup melted butter
1/2 teaspoon vanilla

Mix above ingredients with:

2/3 cup chopped nuts

1 cup chopped figs

Spread batter into 9 x 9 inch pan. Bake at 350° for 45 minutes.

Mushroom Caps

Two pounds fresh mushrooms, stemmed (reserve)

2 eggs

2 cups parmesan cheese, grated

1/4 teaspoon tarragon

2 cups bread crumbs

Chopped reserve mushroom stems

Salt and pepper to taste

Clean and dry mushroom caps and lay on a parchment covered baking sheet, open side up. Combine remaining ingredients in a bowl and fill each mushroom cap, mounding the filling in the center. Sprinkle with a little extra Parmesan cheese. Bake at 350° about 10 minutes, until bubbling and golden. Serve immediately.

Banana Cake

1 cup sifted cake flour

1/2 teaspoon baking powder

1/2 teaspoon salt

1/2 lemon, juiced and zested

6 eggs

1 cup sugar

Filling & Frosting

11/4 cups milk

1/3 cup sugar

3 tablespoons flour

1/8 teaspoon salt

1 egg

1 tablespoon lemon juice

2 ripe bananas

1 cup heavy cream, whipped

1 banana, sliced

Preheat oven to 325°

For Cake:

Sift flour with baking powder and salt. Grate and squeeze lemon.

Separate eggs and beat the yolks until thick as mayonnaise. Gradually work in the sugar, beating until mixture is thick and fluffy. Stir in the lemon juice and half the zest.

Beat egg whites until they form stiff peaks. Carefully fold about half the egg whites into sugar mixture. Do not beat. Fold remaining egg whites into sugar mixture alternately with flour, ending with flour.

Pour batter into two sprayed 8 inch cake pans and bake 50 minutes. Allow to cool in pans before turning out.

Filling:
Scald milk in a saucepan. Sift the sugar, salt and flour together and stir into the hot milk. Beat the egg slightly. Stir a little of the hot milk into the egg, then combine the two (do it this way to avoid curdling the egg). Cook over very low heat, or over a double boiler, stirring constantly, or until custard is heavy. Remove from heat and cool. Stir in lemon juice and sliced bananas.

Cover one cake with the cooled Banana Cream Filling, place the other cake on top. Whip the cream and frost the cake with it. Arrange sliced banana on the top. If not serving immediately, refrigerate.

Gloria

December 23rd, 1951

Darling One of my Life,

*Tonight after dinner I was so cagey — felt all penned up, needed something and didn't know quite what is was, even went to the piano and blundered around, and finally, it came to me. Music. Good music. Your music — that was what I wanted and needed. The only thing I could find was the Mendelsohn Concerto #1 in G Minor, put it on the record player, turned on one light in the living room, got a cup of coffee, a piece of **Spice Cake** and a cigarette and sat down by myself for a few minutes of quiet repose and reflection and found a bit of solace.*

Perfect Spice Cake

2 1/4 cups sifted cake flour
1 teaspoon baking powder
3/4 teaspoon baking soda
1 teaspoon salt
3/4 teaspoon cloves
3/4 teaspoon cinnamon
Pinch of black pepper
3/4 cup butter, softened
3/4 cup firmly packed brown sugar
1 cup granulated sugar
1 teaspoon vanilla
3 eggs
1 cup buttermilk

Sift flour, measuring carefully. Sift again with baking powder, baking soda, salt and spices. Sift or roll out any lumps in the brown sugar. Beat in softened butter until it looks like whipped cream. Work in the brown sugar a little at a time. Now work in the regular sugar a little bit at a time. Add vanilla. Continue creaming until the mixture is very fluffy and the grains of sugar almost disappear. This takes a few minutes, but it is key to the **Perfect Spice Cake**.

When the sugar is all in, add the eggs, one at a time, beating after each addition. Add flour mixture a little bit at a time, alternating with buttermilk, ending with flour. Pour batter into 2 sprayed 8 inch cake pans. Bake 30-35 minutes at 350°, or until cakes edges leave the sides of the pans. Remove from ovens. Allow to cools about five minutes before turning out onto racks to cool thoroughly.

Frost with:
Seven Minute Sea Foam Frosting

2 egg whites, unbeaten
1 1/2 cups firmly packed brown sugar
Dash of salt
1/3 cup water
1 teaspoon vanilla

Cook egg whites, brown sugar and salt in the top of a double boiler, beating constantly about seven minutes, or until frosting stands up in stiff peaks. Remove from boiling water and add vanilla. Beat one minute or until thick enough to spread. Makes enough frosting to cover top and sides of two 8 inch layers or about 2 dozen cupcakes.

Gloria, continued

Martin and Glory were watching Capt. Video on TV, but the music drew Martin downstairs. When he came into the room he said, "I thought that was Daddy playing — it sounds like him," which changed my mood to sadness. I did feel so close to you. Now, I feel so far from you. I hold dear your music and my deep respect for you, your own self.

I could never have loved a man who was "average." I am lucky that a man who is so much would love me.

Thank you, my very own. May God Bless You and Keep You for Me

"Gloria's Gloria"
Swedish Almond Cookies

Swedish cooks are world-renowned for supreme cookie baking. Use whole almonds in the dough, then cut through it with a knife to chop the nuts slightly. Almond slices give a decorative pattern when these rich, crisp cookies are sliced and baked.

Sift....1 1/3 cups flour
1 teaspoon double acting baking powder
1/2 teaspoon salt

Cream together....1/2 cup butter
1/2 cup sugar

Add....1 unbeaten egg
1 tablespoon molasses; Beat well.

Blend in the dry ingredients gradually. Turn out onto a lightly floured board. Add 1/2 cup whole, un-blanched almonds. Form into a ball. Cut through dough with a sharp knife to chop nuts. Knead dough into a ball to distribute nuts evenly.

Place:
on parchment and shape into a roll 2 inches in diameter. Wrap in parchment. Chill at least two hours or overnight.

Cut:

Into 1/8 inch slices and place on a baking sheet covered with parchment.

Bake:

In moderately hot oven (400°) 8-10 minutes, or until golden brown.

Gloria
The Farm
Christmas Night, 1951

My Dear One,

All are in bed, except Yours Truly. I am having a bit of a "Blue, Blue Christmas," just like Ernest Tubb, who sings just for me on the radio right now, I know this. I am at the pantry desk with a cup of tea, the lights lowered. Alone, finally, after a people-and-event-filled day. The kids are in bed upstairs here in the Big House, scrunched two-each in the twin beds in Little Jon and T's tiny attic room. I say they are in bed, but I'll bet you a million dollars they are not asleep.

The Christmas Tree fills the Living Room, floor to ceiling, white tipped in fake snow, covered with Marnie's favorite blue lights, white silk ornaments and white doves. She tied wide blue satin bows on the ends of select branches. Our own little tree in the Cottage, with our little collection of mix and match ornaments, was all but eclipsed by the brilliance of this spectacle!

There were fourteen of us this evening - Marnie, Dad, Glory, Martin, Flossie, Bessie, Lincoln, Mark, Mr. Talbot, Tournier and Big Jon, Little Jon and T, Jr. And me. After a big crazy buffet dinner of Roast Beef, **Yorkshire Pudding***, Gravy, Peas, Mashed Potatoes, Ambrosia, Pie and all the sweets and candy in the world, the four cousins were all wound up! Presents, paper, ribbon, boxes, a couple of dolls, clothing, toys: a grand old mess! Mother's living room never quite looked like that before!*

Martin loves his little train set — smart of you to think of it.
He will concentrate for hours on this one thing. Just like him.
Glory is so cute in new red fuzzy slippers with turned-up toes.
We all missed you, and spoke of you. I do, indeed,
wish you were here.
Me

Yorkshire Pudding/Popovers
6 eggs
Pinch salt
2 1/4 cups milk
3 1/2 cups flour
4 tablespoons melted butter
1 tablespoon maple syrup or brown sugar

The evening before you plan to bake your pudding (or Popovers — same batter) blend the eggs and salt in a food processor. Add 1/2 the flour, 1/2 the milk and blend. Add second half of each and blend. Add melted butter and maple syrup. Blend well. Pour into pitcher and place in fridge overnight. This is very important, since the batter needs time to cure for good rising capabilities. The mistake most people make is making the batter and using it right away.

When ready to bake, *preheat* the baking pan (for Yorkshire pudding, use a glass, 9 x 12 inch pan, for popovers, a heavy cast iron pan is best, but muffin pans do work!) in the 350° oven for about ten minutes. Spray the pan well, and pour the *cold* batter into the pan. (If making Popovers preheat a muffin or popover pan, remove from heat, spray and fill). Bake at 350° for about 40 minutes, until puffed and golden and cooked through. When you remove the Yorkshire Pudding or Popovers from the oven, pierce with a skewer to release the steam so there is no collapse.

So, these are the four most important things to remember about Yorkshire Pudding or Popovers:
- make the batter the day before and keep chilled;
- preheat the oven with the pan in it; then spray;
- add the *cold* batter and put it back in the oven immediately
- When removing from the oven, pierce Popovers or Yorkshire Pudding with a skewer to release the steam

Trust me. This is the key to perfect Popovers or Yorkshire Pudding.

"Gloria's Gloria"
Russian Tea Cakes
2 1/4 cups all-purpose flour
1/4 teaspoon salt

1 cup (2 sticks) butter, softened
1/2 cup powdered sugar
1 teaspoon vanilla extract
3/4 cup finely chopped and toasted hazelnuts
Powdered sugar

Sift flour and salt together. With electric mixer, cream butter in large bowl until light. Gradually add 1/2 cup sugar and beat until fluffy. Add vanilla. Mix in dry ingredients 1/3 at a time. Mix in hazelnuts. Refrigerate at least 1 hour or overnight.

Preheat oven to 400°. Form dough into 1-inch balls. Place 1 inch apart on ungreased cookie sheet. Bake until just firm to touch, about 15 minutes. Transfer to rack and cool slightly. Roll in powdered sugar. Cool completely. Roll cookies in powdered sugar again. Store in airtight container.

Crumb Topping for Muffins & Pies

2 cups organic, unbleached white flour
1 cup cold,unsalted butter
1 cup sugar
1 teaspoon cinnamon

Blend all ingredients in food processor until crumbly, less than a minute. (Do not over blend - will become too doughy.) Store in airtight plastic container in refrigerator or freezer. Sprinkle liberally on top of muffin batter or on unbaked pies or apples prepared for baking.

James
Christmas in Korea

All in all, not a bad Christmas
Got letters and packages from home
Thank you so much,
You Little Darling, for all the goodies-
And all the cookies!
The lads are jealous.
What careful packing,
So few crumbled cookies
Clever girl, to package them in new socks
Guarding them closely
Shall I share a few?
I played for the Catholic midnight mass
An organ, not in good shape, I sounded like
I was playing for a Charlie Chaplin movie

New AG action job,
Right in the thick of things —

James
31 Dec, 1951

So it is bourbon!
I confess,
The veiled remarks were lost on me
So, I used some wonderful bourbon
For SugarShave — but only twice,
Because I didn't like the new formula!
I am now the laughing-stock of the office.

New job, some top secret changes.
Can't discuss them.

For the New Year, a wish for peace
And that all husbands
May be together with wives
And fathers with children.

Mail will be spotty for a bit.

Dark Sage

My imaginary friend Dark Sage came to me in a dream. He took me for walks by the streams, and guided my footsteps on paths through dangerous woods.

I never questioned anyone about this - it seemed so natural to have an Indian in my head.

I asked for my first pair of moccasins. "HoneyBaby!" Gloria exclaimed. "Little girls wear black patent leather Mary Jane's with white anklets. And Keds. And saddle shoes at school. Not moccasins."

"But I like moccasins," I said.

"How do you know you like moccasins?" she crooned in her honey voice.

"I *don't* **know**. But, I've seen them in Martin's Boys' Life Magazine. They look... soft."

So, Gloria, against her own sense of style for little girls, went to the Country Store and found some soft moccasins, and said I could wear them after school.

In the Spring, I made little fires in the late afternoon up on the Kickapoo Mound. I mean *teeny little fires* that absolutely no one would *ever* see, with toothpicks and strips of paper and Strike Anywhere matches I filched from the Barn and struck on rocks.

There I would sit, in shorts and a T-shirt (and moccasins!), no socks, cross-legged in front of my miniscule fire. I'd imagine Dark Sage sitting there with me. I was Little Feather, Princess of the Mound. Sometimes I'd let T come along on my little excursions into the woods, but I didn't tell her about Dark Sage. He was mine. T was sworn to secrecy about my tiny fires.

And then, Harmon Cobb wandered up the path and saw me, tending my tinder.

Busted.

My **Fire Tending** studies commenced.

Harmon Cobb

My grandfather, a businessman who visited his Farm to get grounded, loved horses and riding and seeing his family flit about on 200 acres. He was a city boy with a bunch of land to flit upon.

Cobb's Corner? *That* was about *ground* and what you could *grow* or *raise* on it! Harmon Cobb's cows stood in long lines inside the Milk Barn, swishing their tails while Harmon squeezed their udders. He pushed big draft horses that pulled the soil tillers; had all kinds of tractors and machinery de farm; his barnyard was filled with chickens, geese and ducks, and, in summer, he tended fields and fields of corn that waved long green sleeves in the sun.

Harmon's land met the Sugar Farm at the base of the Kickapoo Mound, a four-mile snake of earth and woods that preserved the bones of the Kickapoo ancestors.

One could never guess by the general farm-boy attitude and appearance that Harmon Cobb was a retired Air force Pilot. The Quonset hut hangar for his Beechcraft Bonanza butted up to the back of the Milking Barn, from which stretched a long, dirt runway around and behind the Sugar Farm, along the boundary of the Kickapoo Mound. From the Big house screened porch, we watched Harmon perform take-offs and landings — on a good day, going *and* coming, he'd make it under the telephone wires that stretched across the far end of the runway, and sail in, smooth as glass. *Over the wires:* he considered that a bumpity, bumpity failure.

I learned important things from Harmon Cobb: how to build a foolproof fire and how to cook corn on the cob were just two.

That day, Harmon took me to his woodpile — for a brief moment I thought he was going to spank me! But, he just made me promise to never build a fire near dry grass, to dig wide areas of dirt around a little pit before laying a fire, and to stay away from buildings or animals. That worked wonders in organizing my mind around building fires. He didn't reprimand me- just taught me how.

"Yer a good listener," he said to me, "and I know yer careful, so's I'm gonna give you this advice about fires." (Sounded like *fahrs*, but I *was* listening!)

"This here pile of wood is a well-seasoned mix of oak and pine — quick burnin' pine to get started, hard, long burnin' oak to keep it goin'. This over here is nice, dry kindling — bigger than your little sticks there, but more effective. Lay 'em down first to get yer fahr goin'.

"You keep to yer little sticks for now. And, I'd suggest — not on the Mound. Mebbe in the dirt there."

"OK", I said.

James

Jan 6

Hey.

This won't be much of a letter.

I've got a cold and feel lousy.

Also, there is too much confusion around here

To be able to concentrate.

Got your letter describing Christmas.

Now that was a letter.

And picture of kids with Santa Claus.

Glory has grown so in six months!

Last night I got exposed to a piano

For the first time since coming to the Far East

Wonderful!

In the place where we are going,

There is even an electric organ in the chapel!

How I long for you.

A Fire Tender's Kit

Wood - *a well-seasoned, good mix of hardwoods (oak, eucalyptus, etc.) and quick-burners like pine*

Split kindling

(and/or a good little hatchet and small dry boards or pieces (make friends with Contractors!) to split into kindling yourself, which is very Girl Scout and feels really good as part of the basic skill set for fire-tending. One must be very careful splitting kindling — always wear gloves, always brace the piece of wood to be split on a flat board to steady it, and always remove your hand from the held piece before hacking at it.)

-Newspaper

-Little rolls of newspaper, dipped in paraffin or candle stubs or

-Cheap or half-used tea lights, metal bottom removed

-Matches or a lighter

Place a small log end out on each side of the grate, if you're using a fireplace — if this fire is in a pit, just place the two straight and steady hardwood logs (inside the lovely two-foot diameter rock ring you have built for your pit) perpendicular to each other with about a foot of space in between. Loosely pack crumpled newspaper (paper bags and newsprint with color really don't work) between logs. Place kindling across base logs, add small pine or quick burner logs to form a square stack like a log cabin, place a piece of crumpled newspaper on top (this is key).

Light the top newspaper first, then light all the rest — this will draw the fire upward, just like a firestorm. If your wood is wet or hard to start, place several paraffin logs or candle stubs on top of your square or log cabin of wood. When the paper is lit, the candle pieces or paraffin logs will melt on the kindling and give the fire a boost. Harmon told me about rubbing two sticks together, too, but I've never had to use the method.

When Harmon started my Fire Tending tutelage, I am sure I heard him say to me, "Always make lots of room for Ox Jeans." Harmon helped me perfect a fire. Many barbeque pits and campfires later, I can say I have rarely fizzled a fire.

James
8 Jan, 1952
Still Cold in da nose.
Miss you terribly
Too punk to write more.

8 Jan later

Have your three wonderful letters.

Wonderful and saddening

At the same time,

Because they are filled with reports

Of little things happening at home

Don't get me wrong,

I wish to know those things.

It is a kind of torture,

But I *want* you to tell me about

Martin's asking Slick Johnson to be his Proxy Daddy!

Now, I know how you feel about gambling,

But I sent you some more money orders.

No comment on the source.

I have my bronchitis cough,

Eternal hacking and blowing.

Sorry to complain.

The Red Books

The red leather recipe binders, embossed in gold with Gloria's name and food categories (Bread-Cakes-Cookies, Meat-Fish-Poultry) smell half way between cinnamon and dust. There are six, each with a mildly musty quality from long storage and pages fingerprinted in chocolate and oil from years of use. Gloria, Flossie and Bessie's souls leap into the kitchen. I revere them. It's a beam of light into the 50s, in the language, the different styles in which the recipes were written, even in the typography on ideas slipped in from magazines or the backs of flour sacks — and there are as many references to cake mixes, Jello and shortcuts as to the homemade meals my memory serves on my plate.

Corn on the Cob

It's a simple thing, this corn business. Harmon took his corn seriously, like everything he did.

In his plaid shirts and overalls, hair parted in the middle and slicked back with Brylcreem, a kind of a grown up Little Rascals' Alfalfa, cowlick and all, he said to me in his slow, deliberate twang, "GloryHoney, it's like this: Getcher water boilin'. Go pick the corn. Shuck it in the field. If you drop a piece, throw it raht away. It's too old. Go home. Treat the corn kindly on the way. Only needs cookin' for three minutes. That's it, Honey. Take this on home and tell yer ma, this here corn is sweet as pie. Butter and Salt."

Gloria

Jan 14

My Own,

*Martin and Glory are both well. She is … independent! will not
tolerate anyone raising their voice to her. She says "Don't talk
to me like that," and means it! Love that.*

Bodes well for her future.

*Martin says to tell you he has two new lower teeth and one
loose upper one and that he is saving for a double holster.
He tried to save a woodchuck from a fight it had lost with
Major, but the woodchuck died. I hear Martin took it to the
Bunkhouse, where he and Slick relieved the dead woodchuck
of its teeth. Your Martin questioned me this morning - why
the tooth fairy did not take the woodchuck's offering! I looked
under the pillow, and sure enough! There were four slimy,
rather black, rotten, snaggly-looking teeth under there.*

*Time to put these two to bed and settle myself down to
my favorite sport — watching television. Never thought I'd
succumb, but it's an opiate for a lonely heart. May God Bless
You and Keep you for Me*

The Dairy Barn

Twenty cows were in Harmon's care and employ, hand-milked twice a day, every day, 365 days a year. Tails swishing, moos exhaling, morning and night. Harmon and Ralph milked the "girls" - Martin and I liked to keep them company, especially for the evening ritual. We were not often up before light.

Harmon sat on the same side of the cows each day.

"Rootine, Darlin'." he said. "Makes 'em happy cows."

The "girls" all had their names and a number on a little metal tag attached to the left ear, like an exotic, dangly earbob. He'd pick up a flapping ear, squint at the tag and say, "Maggie. Come on ol' girl," or "Come along, ol' thing, ol' Dottie." He'd place his little three-legged stool at a right angle to a cow and sit with his head resting on her flank. He'd wash the udder with warm water and clean cloth and place a pail under her teats. Twice every day. He taught us how to squeeze a teat ever so gently at the top with our thumb and forefinger to force milk into a stream.

We'd collect fresh, steaming froth in large, covered milk cans, and haul them home in our little red wagon, wobbling down the dirt path that connected the farms.

James
Jan 15th, 1952

Just a quick note to let you know
I am not lost
All confusion around here

Butter

Flossie and Gloria reserved about a gallon of cream a week for butter, putting 1 quart at a time into a bowl for mixing. A churn slowly agitates cream causing it to thicken and then break into butter particles, leaving buttermilk behind. A mixer is a little on the wild side and must be used carefully and slowly, so not to mix too much of the buttermilk into the butter. It also tends to splatter on faces and clothes... so they covered the bowl and mixer with a dishtowel.

The butter particles gather together. Flossie removed it in a lump from the bowl, reserving the buttermilk for Lincoln, and set it aside as Gloria mixed more cream into butter.

Then they would rinse out the remaining buttermilk. While Gloria worked the butter in her hands, Flossie gently poured lukewarm water over it. They kept pressing the clear water out with hands or a paddle.

While they were kneading, they added canning salt, about 1 teaspoon per pound of butter. I have used kosher salt.

After forming the butter into balls or pressing into molds, Bessie wrapped it in parchment paper for refrigerating or freezing. (When we first arrived at the Farm in 1951, Pop had just received shipment of a new electric refrigerator/freezer for the Big House Kitchen. He moved the old, Victorian oak icebox to the cottage, where, for several years, we received delivery of ice once a week from Harold Green, who wore a tattered leather apron and pulled his giant chunks of ice out of his truck with huge tongs. He'd plunk the behemoth block of ice into the drawer above the icebox door.)

Fresh Farmer Cheese
Use pasteurized, instead of ultra-pasteurized, if available. Fresh raw milk is great, too!
I was part owner of a cow on Benbow Road — but that comes much later

3 half gallons whole milk

2 quarts buttermilk

1 1/2 teaspoon salt

Cheese cloth

Preparation:

Over low heat, slowly heat the milk in a heavy-bottomed pot, stirring often, until it is just about to simmer. Stir in the buttermilk, and turn off the heat. Stir slowly with wooden spoon until the milk begins separate into curds (solids) and whey (liquid). Let stand for 10 minutes. Stir in the salt.

Line a large strainer with 2 layers of cheesecloth, and place over a stockpot to catch the whey. Ladle the curds into the cheesecloth, and let the whey drain for 10 minutes. Gather up the edges of the cheesecloth, and form a knot or bundle at the top. Tie the string to a wooden spoon or dowel, and hang the cheese curds over the stockpot and continue draining for 30 minutes for soft cheese, or overnight for hard cheese.

After draining, remove the cheese from the cloth, and transfer into a container and refrigerate. This fresh cheese can be used for up to 5 days. Use as a spread, or as you would use cream cheese, or cottage cheese if it is soft, or cut into pieces if you have made hard cheese.

Gloria

Jan 16

Wish I could send you some of **Flossie's Fresh Cheese**, *which I know you love. Wish I could say I have been in good spirits, too. Should I tell you how lonely and blue I am? I don't know. I don't want to upset you and yet you know me well enough to realize I can't hide my feelings even in writing. Maybe especially in writing. There is only one thing wrong with me and that is your absence and don't let anyone tell you that time makes it better.*

May God Bless you and keep you for Me

A Coop of Chickens

Lincoln's little rickety Coop was hard-pressed to hold 32 Rhode Island Reds, which we gave names like Little Red Hen, Chicken Little, Marion, Sparkle Plenty, Hoboken, Frances and Sam. We could tell them apart. Really! The two roosters, Robin Hood and Friar Tuck, didn't get along, but bonded in their general mistrust of all humans, even Lincoln. Robin Hood and Friar Tuck stalked us in the long narrow coop, scruffling and scrabbling their way through the layers of straw and poop, racing to our turned backs to peck at our heels, scattering hens in all directions squawking, "Ack Ack Begack!" Chickens squabble, they are stupid, they crash around like, like chickens — and there is nothing prettier or tastier than the orange yolks of homegrown eggs.

James
18 Jan, 1952
I must snatch a minute
Only have a minute
To tell you I love you.
Your beautiful eyes
Have been haunting me all day,
Possibly because
I dreamed of you last night —
A brief, fleeting glimpse of you,
But you looked wonderful.

Flossie's Custard

5 egg yolks

2 whole eggs

one cup sugar

1 teaspoon vanilla

3 cups scalded milk

Beat eggs, sugar and vanilla. Pour in milk. Pour into casserole or individual custard cups. Sprinkle with nutmeg. Place casserole in a pan of hot water. Bake at 300°, 35-60 minutes. Done when knife comes out clean.

Cheese Soufflé

Preheat oven to 350°

8 eggs, separated

3 cups milk, scalded

6 tablespoons butter

6 tablespoons flour

3 cups shredded Gruyere cheese

1/2 cup shredded Parmesan cheese

3 tablespoons softened butter

3 tablespoons grated Gruyere

Melt butter in sauce pan. Add flour and blend, making a smooth roux. Pour in scalded milk, constantly stirring and smoothing. Simmer until slightly thickens and coats the back of a wooden spoon. Remove from heat and add egg yolks, one at a time, until blended. Cook one minute. Remove from heat, add Gruyere and cool completely.

Beat egg whites until firm. Fold in a few spoonsful of cheese mixture to egg whites, then add whites to cheese mixture. Coat the bottom and sides of soufflé dish with softened butter and sprinkle with remaining grated cheese. Gently pour cheese and egg mixture into soufflé dish. Sprinkle with Parmesan cheese. Place in hot oven and bake, undisturbed for about forty minutes, until golden and very firm. Remove from oven and serve immediately, before it collapses. Makes 2-4 servings. The cheese on the outside forms a luscious crust.

Or follow all the same directions, but use a 9x12 inch glass casserole dish. The soufflé will be thinner, but will have more surface area and more crusty bits.

Farm Frittata

2 tablespoons butter or olive oil
2 cups diced potatoes
1/4 cups chopped onion (Yellow or green)
1 cup yellow or white corn
8 eggs, beaten and blended with
1/4 cup half and half
1 cup shredded cheese
Grated Parmesan cheese

Sauté potatoes and onion in oil until golden. Remove from pan. Sauté corn in butter until golden. Add to potato and onion mixture. Using a non-stick spray, coat a glass 9 x 12 casserole dish. Pour egg and half and half mixture into casserole dish, sprinkle with vegetables and shredded cheese, carefully blending into eggs. Sprinkle top with grated Parmesan. Bake at 325° for about 30 minutes, or until set and golden. Serve immediately.

Gloria
Jan 18th, 1952

Money orders are being sent pronto to savings. Wonderful to be building a nest-egg. No other comment on their origins.

I know how difficult it must be for you without good music. I'm shying away from music until I can do it with you. Can't listen to an organ, can't even enter a church, since I know I would break down completely. I only hope that God understands my weakness and will forgive me.

Glory! How I wish you could see Glory. She grows more inquisitive every day and is so lovable. Sister Dennis told me she was the most affectionate child she has ever seen.

I made **Floating Islands** *for her today, one of her favorites. She gets such a kick out of the names of things, and turned the* **Floating Island** *into a long story about people lost on a dessert island — yes, dessert island - of snow!*

Last night when I was leaving their room Martin said to me, "Say, Mama, I sure would like to know the story of how you got to be our mother." It was 9 o'clock (he gets to stay up on Thursday nights to watch Amos 'n Andy, which he dearly loves), so I said "It's too late for stories." He said, "Well, I am sleepy, but you will tell me tomorrow." Since he never forgets anything, I'll find out today just what story it is he wants to hear.

218

Floating Islands

Custard
2 vanilla beans, split length-wise
2 cups whole milk
6 large egg yolks
1/2 cup sugar

Meringues
6 egg whites
One cup sugar

Caramel
1/2 cup sugar
1/4 cup water

For Custard:
Place milk and split vanilla beans in a saucepan and bring to simmer over medium-high heat. Remove from heat, cover, and steep 10 minutes. Scrape insides of vanilla beans into milk.

Whisk yolks and sugar in heavy medium bowl until thick, about 2 minutes. Gradually whisk into warm milk mixture. Stir over medium-low heat (do not boil) until custard thickens and coats the back of a spoon, about 9 minutes. Pour custard into small bowl. Cover and chill until cold, at least 3 hours or up to 2 days.

For Meringues:

Spray 9x12x3-inch pan with nonstick vegetable oil spray. Coat pan lightly with sugar. Using an electric mixer, beat egg whites on high speed In a large bowl to soft peaks. Gradually beat in 1 cup sugar. Beat until stiff and glossy. With a large spoon, place the egg whites in the milk, leave for 2 minutes then turn aside and leave again for 2 minutes. Remove whites from the milk and place on prepared pan.

Bake in 300° oven for 20 minutes. The whites will rise so you need a deep baking dish. Let the meringue cool for half an hour .The meringues can be refrigerated for 2 to 3 hours.

For Caramel:

Stir sugar and 1/4 cup water in heavy small saucepan over medium heat until sugar dissolves. Bring to boil, brushing down sides of pan with wet pastry brush to dissolve any sugar crystals. Boil until syrup is pale golden color, occasionally swirling pan, about 5 minutes. Remove pan from heat. Let syrup cool until thick enough to fall from tines of fork in ribbons, about 8 minutes. (If caramel becomes too thick, rewarm slightly over low heat, stirring constantly.)

Spoon some sauce into center of each plate. Arrange 2 meringues on each. Dip fork into caramel and drizzle over meringues so that caramel comes off in strands that harden in threads. Serve.

James
Jan 19ᵗʰ, 1952
Gripe

Our mail is hopelessly tangled
A letter from you I've not had
The whole situation is mangled
In fact, I am feeling quite bad.

It isn't your fault, Little Darlin'
For the action occurring precludes
A constantly flowing good contact;
But a mail lack gives me the moods.

By the time that you get this epistle
I'll have gotten some dozens, I hope,
Of letters from the pen of my dearest,
If I ain't I'll just piss up a rope!

However, there's much consolation,
For soon I can hear your sweet voice
And if waiting a few days means talking
To you, it's obviously my choice.

I hope that you haven't a-fretted
For busier than Hell I have been
But regular writing I'm doing
From now till we meet once again.

My forte is actually poetry,
I talk, so it seems, best in verse,
However, my style needs a buffing
For it's gradually getting quite worse.

When I come home
Will you make **Baked Alaska**?
I'll ask ya!

Baked Alaska

1 pound cake, frozen

(see recipe for Forget-Me-Not-Cake, page 42

- bake in loaf pan and freeze)

1 quart good quality strawberry ice cream

6 egg whites

1/4 teaspoon fresh lemon juice

3/4 cup sugar

Cut frozen cake crosswise into 1/2-inch-thick slices. Make a box of cake slices, inside of which is the block of ice cream. Completely cover the ice cream with the cake slices. Freeze at least 25 minutes.

Preheat oven to 450°.

Beat egg whites and a pinch of salt with an electric mixer until foamy, then add lemon juice and continue to beat until whites hold soft peaks. Gradually add sugar, beating, and continue beating until whites just hold stiff, glossy peaks.

Remove ice-cream and cake block from freezer and mound meringue over it, spreading all around cake. Bake in middle of oven until golden brown, about 6 minutes. Serve immediately.

The block may be assembled 2 days ahead and frozen, tightly wrapped.

Gloria

Jan 27th

My Own,

Sunday afternoon, everyone is quietly occupied — I have retired to my room behind closed doors to have a few moments to re-read your letters.

Children all up and down with a virus but on the mend.

Thanks for noticing — 16 pounds. Just cutting down on portions and desserts. Eating lots of salad.

*Martin asks, "What's **Baked I'll Ask Ya**?"*

Crème Brulee

2 cups heavy cream

One vanilla bean, split

4 egg yolks

4 tablespoons sugar

3-4 tablespoons light brown sugar

Place cream and vanilla bean in saucepan and heat to to scalding. Beat egg yolks until thick. Scrape vanilla bean and add to milk. Slowly stir hot cream into egg and sugar mixture. Pour into a 1 quart or six individual baking dishes or ramekins. Place in a pan of hot water and bake at 350° for about 40 minutes or until a knife inserted in the middle comes out clean. Chill about one hour. When serving, sprinkle top or tops with brown sugar and place under broiler for a few minutes until sugar melts. Watch carefully, because sugar burns easily.

Gloria

Jan 28th

Darling One,

Today I received a call from the Red Cross.

Well, it appeared to be the Red Cross.

First, she asked for Mrs. Sugar and wanted to know if a Mrs. James worked here. A baker? she thought.

She shmumbled over her words and stumbled over the form or notes from which she was reading. I came to the line after a confused handing of the phone from Flossie to Marnie to Flossie to me.

"Mrshes. Jamesh?," she asked.

"No, but I am Mrs. James R. Baker. Are you perhaps looking for me?"

"Do you bake?"

"Well, uhm, yes, but that is our last name."

"Oh. You're all right, then."

"All right?"

"Yesh, not sick. No problemsh?"

"Who is this?"

"I am Mrsh. Brown, from the Red Crosh. Your husband — is that your hushband, that Mr. James?"

"Mr. James Baker."

"Yes, Mr. James, the baker."

"No! Oh! Is he all right? Is that why you are calling me? Has something happened?"

"No, no. At least, not known to me. I don't know. He wanted us to call you."

226

And more like this. Oh, my own, tell me no bad thing has happened to you.
I think and hope the woman was skunked!
Please let me know of your well-being.

James
Jan 29th, 1952

Sonnet
To say that I have missed you, dear
Would be an understatement;
And at the present time there seems
No danger of abatement.

That is to say there's little chance
That we'll together be
In body soon, but spirit-wise
You're more than close to me.

For in the union that we have
There is that subtle thing
Which binds us tightly ever and
Helps take away the sting

Of separation, howe'er long.
Pray God He'll help us keep it strong.
…Me

Gloria
Jan 31st, 1952

Martin now down with measles, Dad down with what I hope is the flu, Mother in Kansas, Dr. is giving all children measles shots.
Just found that original **Green Goddess Dressing** *recipe we were looking for six months ago!*
Me

Green Goddess Dressing

George Arliss (1868-1946), a prominent English stage star, was staying at The Palace Hotel *in San Francisco in 1923 during the run of a play called "The Green Goddess" (by William Archer). In preparing for a banquet in Mr. Arliss' honor, the Executive Chef of the hotel used an array of chopped green herbs to suggest the name of the play.* **Green Goddess Dressing** *became the hotel's signature salad dressing and has been served in the hotel's Garden Court Restaurant since that time. Goes well with seafood salads, particularly crab.*

On a date, after a walk around Union Square and Chinatown, James splurged and took Gloria to the Palace Hotel Garden Court for lunch, where they fell in love with **Green Goddess Dressing**.

The original recipe:
1 garlic clove
2 cups of mayonnaise
4 minced anchovy fillets
1 green onion, chopped
2 teaspoons chopped parsley
2 teaspoons chopped chives
1 Tablespoon tarragon vinegar (or to taste)
!/4 teaspoon dried OR 1 teaspoon cut, fresh tarragon
Toss ingredients in food processor and give it a whirl!

Pour over salad greens, watercress, or seafood salad.

James
Feb 1ˢᵗ, 1952
Got the Red Cross Report I asked for
Stating all was well with you.
Thought you might not be hearing from me
So I asked for the report
So you would at least know I was alive
Hope I didn't upset you.

Love knowing about Martin's school activities.
Some [of his papers] seem right-handed,
Some left.
Are the nuns trying to change him?
I am returning his papers herewith because
One destroys everything here
To travel light —
And these
I can't bring myself to tear up.
I memorize every word
Of your wonderful letters
Before I burn them.
What a comfort you are.

I am panting to hear
What finally came of Martin's question
About how you got to be his mother!
I wish he had been able to ask *me*.
I would have told him

That his daddy searched for a long time
To find a girl whose heart
Was made of solid gold —
Whose body was made
Of peaches and cream —
Whose mind was fashioned
Of the best of all —
And about whom God said
"And this is my Best —
I will throw away the mold."
After searching
And looking
And hunting
And trying
And making mistakes —
I finally found that girl —
And that
Is how you got to be
His mother.
And I sure am glad.
Me

Gloria
Sunday the 5th

*Ahh, I feel virtuous — I have just completed my six **Red Recipe Binders** — organized, catalogued and complete! Dad was happy to see I'd put his gift to use.*

Gloria sat at the Pantry desk in the quiet evening writing to James. She had been still for some minutes, imagining his **Baked Alaska** kiss on her lips. The light was low, the little lamp casting a yellow glow over the surface of the desk and half-cast an orange halo over Gloria's blonde head. She heard a whispery, scratching sound to her left and looked up.

"Ack! Uh! Oh Lord!" she shouted as a rather large mouse scampered across her foot to the open cellar door. She leaped to the side, too late to save her stocking, and tripped over the braided rug, catching herself on the back of a chair. Gloria was known to whack at rodents, but, no broom handy, she watched it scamper down the steps.

Lincoln came running down the Backstairs, bat in hand, thinking Miss Gloria had got herself burgled!

They set up six mouse traps and covered all the jars and baskets. Life on the Farm.

Gloria continued
Monday noon-

Hello again — I was driven out of the kitchen by one of my little friends with a long tail, and by the time I was through with that little drama, and got upstairs I was too tired to finish this last night.
Got your poem today —you take away loneliness and make tears at the same time.
I love you, old thing.
More than anything, more than all there is.
Me

James
Feb 5ᵗʰ 1952
Aboard the USS Pick

Hello dearest.
I won't attempt to chronicle this
Like before. No notebook, anyway
Slept for four hours — in my clothes
Loaded on trucks for drive to Inchon
Bitter wind. Below zero temp
Breakfast on board — flapjacks and bacon
First good cakes I've had since 44ᵗʰ Ave
White tablecloth, silver, good coffee
Ship better in appointments
Than my friend in September
Bunk good.
Head clean.
Everything fine
On the way to Japan
Will be able to talk to you —
And will be away from combat zone
And closer to coming home

Gloria

Thurs Feb 7

*Thanks for clearing up the Red Cross thing. I was confused
because you should have been receiving my letters.
I read Martin your story about how I came to be his mother.
He said, "Ah, he saw* **you** *and said, 'Marry me!' Just like that!"
Life is so simple.
I said I thought he had forgotten about it. He said,
"I was giving you time."
As for telling him about the birds and the bees?
You take that one, too.
Gorgeous fairy snow land with bright sunshine today.
But I am beginning to agree with Sinclair Lewis that, "Winter is
not a season, it is an occupation."
Did you know he died in January?
Baby T has the measles. They are all four sneezing, coughing
with runny little noses. So here we go again. It's the weather
— warm with rain, then freezing with snow.
May God keep you and bless you for,
Me.*

Gloria

Feb 9th

My dearest One,

Winter has returned. Zero this morning and my feet are cold.

This big old drafty house takes several days to warm up!

Coming home soon? I'll make your **Baked Sole Thermidor***!*

Baked Sole Thermidor

Lobster Thermidor was given to the world on the evening of January 24, 1894, at Chez Marie, a well-known Paris restaurant, when Victorien Sardou's new play opened at the theatre Comedie-Francais. The restaurant launched its new dish by giving it the name of the play, "Thermidor," named after one of the summer months of the French republican calendar: Thermidor (or Fervidor, from Greek thermon, "summer heat"), starting July 19th or 20th. Among other reforms, the new Republican government sought to institute a new social and legal system, a new system of weights and measures (which became the metric system), and a new calendar, as they tried to sweep away the trappings of the ancien régime; some more successfully than others. Alas, Thermidor failed as a month, but became the name of another sauce.

Gloria preferred sole to lobster

1 1/2 pounds filet of sole
3/4 teaspoon salt
Dash pepper
1/2 cup milk
2 tablespoons butter
2 tablespoons flour
1 cup milk
1 teaspoon sherry
1/4 cup grated Gruyere cheese

Place fish in sprayed 6 x 10 inch baking dish. Salt and pepper and cover with 1/2 cup milk. Bake in 350° oven about 30 minutes. Melt butter. Add flour and make a roux, blending in flour completely before gradually adding remaining milk. Cook over low heat until smooth and thick, stirring. Add sherry and cheese. Pour over fish. Broil until golden.

Gloria

Feb 10th

Dear One,

Children all under-the-weather except our valiant Glory. She helped make a **Burnt Sugar Cake** *and a* **Tuna Tettrazzini Bake** *today — her remedy. She thought those things would be good for "the sick in our home."*

Are we there yet?

Burnt Sugar Cake

2 cups sugar
1/3 cup boiling water
2 1/2 cups cake flour
3 teaspoons baking powder
1/2 teaspoon salt
1/2 cup butter
2 eggs
1 cup milk
1 teaspoon vanilla

Place 3/4 cup of the sugar into a heavy-bottomed saucepan over low heat. Stir until melted and a deep brown color. Remove from heat and add water slowly, while stirring. Return to heat and cook about five minutes, constantly stirring. Cool.

Meanwhile, sift flour, then measure and add baking powder and salt and sift again. Cream butter and gradually add remaining sugar, creaming until light and fluffy. Separate eggs. Add yolks, one at a time, to butter sugar mixture and stir well after each addition. Add four tablespoons of the sugar syrup (the rest goes into the frosting) and blend. Add dry ingredients alternately with milk, about 1/3 at a time, beating after each addition until smooth, ending with flour. Add vanilla. Beat egg whites until stiff and fold into cake mixture. Pour batter into two sprayed 9 inch layer cake pans. Bake at 350° for about 30 minutes.

When cooled completely, cover with:

Burnt Sugar Frosting

1 cup sugar

2 tablespoons water

2 egg whites

2 tablespoons sugar syrup, saved from above

1/8 teaspoon salt

1/2 teaspoon vanilla

Combine sugar, water, egg whites and syrup in the top of a double boiler. Place over boiling water and, beating continuously, cook for seven minutes, or until frosting is thick. Remove from heat, add vanilla, and continue to beat until of spreading consistency.

Tuna Tettrazini-Bake

1/2 onion, chopped

2 carrots, chopped

2 stalks celery, chopped

2 tablespoons butter

3 tablespoons flour

1 cup milk

1/2 teaspoon salt

Dash pepper

1/4 teaspoon paprika

3/4 cup grated cheddar cheese

12 ounces tuna, flaked and drained

2 cups cooked pasta or macaroni noodles

1 cup bread crumbs in 1/4 cup melted butter

Melt butter. Sauté vegetables until soft. Add flour and make a roux, blending in all the flour before gradually adding milk. Cook over low heat to thicken. Add seasonings. Add cheese and melt into sauce. Place tuna and noodles in a sprayed casserole dish and gently toss. Pour sauce over and slightly mix in with tuna and noodles. Sprinkle buttered bread crumbs over the top. Bake at 325°40 minutes to an hour, until the top is golden and the casserole is bubbling in the middle.

Gloria
Mon, Feb 12th

How wonderful to hear your voice! How I managed to speak,
I'll never know — I was so tightly held together.
The irony—1001 things to talk about, and my mind is jelly
when I hear your voice over the phone. I did not wake the
children - I couldn't bear to share these few precious minutes
— I wanted you all to myself this first time! I know you were
disappointed and perhaps it was wrong and selfish of me — I
know how thrilled and excited they would have been — I even
feel a little ashamed now. Forgive me, my darling —
God Bless….

Gloria
Wed, Feb 13th
My Dearest,
My answer to all questions is the same. Come home.
Can hardly wait to hear from you to know of your arrival - I
love you with all my heart. God bless…

James

Japan

Feb 13th, 1952

So good to hear your voice yesterday.

So good

So much to do here.

So much paperwork

Plotting and planning

Will be too busy and occupied

To write much

Nice chapel.

Hammond organ

Doesn't operate well

on the Japanese current,

but I am not complaining.

James

Feb 14th, 1952

Blue Blue Moon

Once in a blue blue moon
A girl comes along in your life

Once in a blue blue moon
The one you will take for a wife

You look and you search
And have empty arms

When the one you are seeking
Is there, on the Farm

Once in a blue blue moon
A girl will have blue blue eyes

Once in a blue blue moon
She'll turn out to be just your size

She looks like an angel
She fits like a glove

You see in her eyes
She's been longing for love

Once in a blue blue moon
She'll look back with that smile on her face

And once in a blue blue moon
You will finally come home to your place

My love on Valentines' Day
From very, very far away

Gloria
Mon, Feb 25th

I am thinking of you sitting there on Valentines' Day, alone on your bunk in a tent at night, writing love poems by lantern light. I am lonesome in a house full of people. I can only imagine how lonely it must be for you, all of you, over there. Alone in a war-zone full of men.

God bless....

Until the Cows Come Home

The oak wall-phone jangled early one morning. Harmon, his voice higher and squeakier than usual, screeched through the receiver, "Cows out! Cows out! Could use some help over heah! Goin' now to the north pasture, by Doo's back line there! Bring people!" he yelled, and hung up with a bang.

Pop knew what to do. He gathered us all, except Flossie, who started making coffee and hot chocolate. We threw on our coats and Wellingtons and piled into the back of the Farm truck, kids bobbing and crashing around in the truck bed, adults wedged together in front, bouncing over back pastures, boomity, boomity, where we found a sloppy scene:

A windy spring rainstorm had broken down a bit of fence-line between the Doolittle's and Cobb's Corner and allowed all twenty of Harmon's milk cows to explore the wide world of fallow pastures. The girls had scattered in the night, some slipping in the mud. One old gal had gotten her tail tangled in the sagging barbed wire. She was straining and mooing up a wonderful great storm of her own.

All those discombobulated moo-ers were headed toward the Doolittle's recently planted field of corn, little tops swishing and waving greenly in the breeze. Yum yum.

"Doo!" My grandfather called. "I'll send my folks 'round to the left!"

"Great! Great! We're goin' to the right!"

250

Harmon, hat askew, went rumbling by on his tractor, herding cows away from corn. He waved to us, calling out a distracted, "Thanks!"

The four cousins took up positions nearest the truck, madly waving our little arms to keep the cows headed away. The Sugar Farm adults fanned out to the left, the Doolittles to the right, forming a human chain between corn and cows. And there were cows everywhere.

It seemed impossible to me, one of the smallest and least effective arm waving cow herders, to corral the meandering, clueless four-legged, swishy-tailed farm girls and get them back to their little pasture by the barn. *What the heck do they know?* I thought. *It just looks like dinner ahead to them!*

But after about an hour's worth of mud slipping, arm waving, general cow calling and coddling ("C'mon old girl. It's all right." "Git up ol' pal. Let's gitcha home here.") we slipped the last of the escapees through the fence-break and back into Harmon's domain.

Harmon and Ralph herded his girls back home. We left Slick to help Mr. Doolittle and Harmon repair the fence. And then we rumbled on home ourselves: cold, wet, dirty and laughing.

Discarding muddy Wellies and jackets on the back porch, we exploded into the warm kitchen, where the fire blazed. A plate of Flossie's **Snickerdoodles** and pitchers of steaming hot chocolate were on the table.

Snickerdoodles

1 1/2 cups sugar

1 cup butter, softened

2 eggs

2 3/4 cups flour

2 teaspoons cream of tartar

1 teaspoon baking soda

1/4 teaspoon salt

1/4 cup sugar

2 teaspoons ground cinnamon

Heat oven to 400°. Mix sugar, softened butter and eggs together in a large bowl. Stir in dry ingredients. Shape dough into balls, about 1 1/4 inches. Roll each ball in the cinnamon and sugar mixture and place on parchment on baking sheet about two inches apart. Bake about ten minutes, or until cracks form on top. Cool on wire racks.

James
Japan
April 20ᵗʰ, 1952

Plans actually being made now
For the change
I will no longer be needed
Or have a job
And my commitment here
Is soon to be UP,
As they say
It's hard to think
The time that seemed so long
Is suddenly over
And I will be coming home
It will take weeks
Or a month
Or more
To crawl across the ocean again
Or find an available plane
Details later
A plane is my first hope as you know
Practice making your **Crepes Suzette**!
I am coming home.

James
May 10, 1952
Onboard the Pomeroy

No book this time,
Just sheaves of loose paper
Scattered notes
For my Beloved

Secret work has no reward
If it takes me away from you
I live in my head and dream my dreams
I stare off into outer space
I wonder if they will give chase
My dreams of you
The Reds in view
The nightmares of this race

My dream of you
Is coming true
I am coming home to you
I'll be with you
And will renew
The wonder of our love
A'dieu! To this war
In this far-off place.

James
May 12ᵗʰ, 1952
Onboard the Pomeroy

Gloria, Gloria, why do I love thee?
Shall I count the whys?

You see I am on a ship
1.   Because your voice sends shivers up my spine

It is full of men returning home
2.   Because you are the most beautiful girl on earth

We are weary of rock, rock, rock
3.   You are mother of my beautiful children

The sea-worthy hope for the best
4.   You cook with the hands of the angels

The land-lovers hope for the john!
5.   You married me in spite of my faults

The food tastes like cardboard
6.   Your lips are as sweet as honey

And yes, we are bored to tears!

Planting a Garden

Gloria marked off the "James Home" days on the calendar. As she practiced her **Crepes Suzette** for his homecoming dinner, Martin, Little Jon, T and I established our mini garden with a few of Lincoln's precious seedlings — six carrots, two tomatoes, six peas, one zucchini squash, one sunflower, one pumpkin plant, which we proposed to grow into a major behemoth Jack O'Lantern. On a little valuable but vacant piece of real estate just inside Lincoln's Garden Gate, we measured off the area — three feet by three feet, marking off a section for the pumpkin plant to spread out along the fence. Lincoln tied sections of white kitchen string around four little straight twigs which we stuck into each corner of our "dirt." We raked the area with kitchen forks, and dug seed rows with soup spoons.

We stopped digging to watch Lincoln and Slick repair the fence that kept Herman, Myrtle, Greta and Git on the outside of the Garden. We heard Lincoln scolding. "Git!" he'd say. "Git… Git!"

Pop and I rode out on ponies for a Spring inspection of the fences that kept Herman, Myrtle, Greta and Git *inside* the Sugar Farm estate.

On a clear bright sun-shiny day, Gloria, Martin and I sat at the picnic table with our lunch — cold roast chicken, **Fresh Mayonnaise**, black olives, cheese, pickles and **French Bread**. We watched as Lincoln, in overalls with pockets stuffed with small tools, distributed his precious seedlings in straight little rows — carrots, peas, beans, squash, onions, leeks, lettuce, pumpkins, tomatoes, sunflowers, potatoes.

Gloria said, "Your Daddy *is* coming home, you know. Do you remember your Daddy?"

"Of course I remember my Daddy," I said, perturbed and precocious, curls bobbing. "He's the only grown-up who doesn't think I am too big to pick up!"

Martin, more dignified in general, said, "Yes, my Daddy understands me. He's the one, my real daddy."

"Oh, he'll be glad to hear that," Gloria remarked with a smile. "He thought you'd defected to Slick Johnson!"

"No," Martin said. "Just friends, we're just buckaroos. No one is like my Daddy." This was coming from someone who was wearing rolled up jeans and a holster.

"Things will be different when Daddy comes home," Gloria said.

"How's that?" I asked, imagining the pleasure of showing him our gi-normous pumpkin and luscious red tomatoes - and getting picked up like a little girl again.

"Well, we'll be our whole family once more, four instead of three."

"Okay," I said.

"A-a-nd, he'll be having breakfast with us every day," she said.

"Right," we said together.

"A-a-nd, he'll be sleeping in my bed," she said, with a shy smile.

We smiled, too, happy to know they'd be together again.

"Okay," we said.

"Does that mean we can't sleep with you anymore?" I asked.

"Not always," she whispered.

"Two's company, three's a crowd, Glory," Martin piped.

"What?"

"And four is woise!" he went on, looking meaningfully at Gloria.

"What?" I repeated.

"They are *married*, silly," he said, like it was public knowledge and everyone knew it but me.

Still not getting it, I asked, "Aren't we all married?"

Gloria maneuvered the subject back to pumpkins.

Fresh Mayonnaise (Aioli)

4 garlic cloves, peeled, chopped fine
2 egg yolks
1/8 teaspoon sea salt
1 cup virgin olive oil
Juice of 1/2 lemon
1/2 teaspoon cold water

Chop up the garlic and salt in the food processor and slowly add the egg yolks. Add in half of the continuing to pulse the food processor slowly so the oil will emulsify and thicken your sauce. Once the first half of the oil is incorporated, add the water and the lemon juice. Slowly add the rest of the oil. The mixture thickens as you continue to blend. If sauce becomes too thick, add a bit more warm water, one teaspoon at a time.

Crepes Suzette
The thinnest, crispiest little pancakes, served at the table aflame!

Crepes:
1 cup flour
1/4 teaspoon salt
2 tablespoons sugar
1/2 teaspoon grated orange rind
2 eggs
1 cup milk
2 tablespoons butter, melted

Sauce:

1/3 cup butter

1 cup powdered sugar

2 tablespoons orange juice

1 teaspoon lemon juice

3 tablespoons white wine

6 tablespoons brandy

Powdered Sugar

To make Crepes:

Mix together flour, salt, sugar and orange rind in a bowl. Beat eggs and blend with milk and melted butter and blend with flour mixture. Butter the bottom of a 5" skillet and place on medium high heat. When sizzling, pour about 3 tablespoons of batter onto the pan, tilting pan around until batter covers the bottom. When the bottom is browned, turn crepe over and quickly brown the other side. Remove from pan, dust with powdered sugar and roll up. Makes 12.

Sauce:

Mix butter and powdered sugar in in a shallow skillet. Stir over very low heat until butter melts. Add orange and lemon juices, orange rind and white wine. Stir until blended and reduce. Place 2 Crepes each in 6 individual, heat proof serving dishes, pour hot sauce over Crepes. Pour brandy over each, set afire and serve.

"Glory Lake"

It was sometime in June before James got through all the paperwork, red tape, closure and traveling it took to get back to the Farm from Japan. In that time, Pop contracted for three bulldozers to dig a big hole out of 3 acres and then filled it from the well to make a lake. It was a 5 minute walk from the Big House, in the old potato patch. He hauled in a floating dock on the back of a giant flatbed truck, had it picked up by a crane and plopped out in the middle of the lake. He made bets with us to see who could make it out to the dock first. I wasn't much of a swimmer, and didn't like the squishy lake-mud between my toes. Martin took to the water like a duck, dog-paddling next to Pop, with Major splashing along beside them. Pop and Martin sat on the floating dock, legs dangling in the water, throwing a stick out into the pond.

"Go, fetch it, boy!" Pop yelled.

"Fetch! Fetch! Fetch it, Major!" Martin got right into the spirit.

I sat pouting at the shore of Little Glory Lake, my consolation the lake named for me, and our **Chicken Salad Sandwiches** and **Chocolate Chip Cookies** in the basket at my side.

By June, there were bright yellow star-like blooms on our tomato plants, scattered with little green pearl-sized fruit. Our pumpkin was just embarking on its road to giant-hood, a good-sized blue-green nob emerging from the one golden flower we had left on the plant in our careful pruning.

I didn't get it then, but Gloria was nervous about James' return. Separated almost a year! When she was an older woman, she still blushed to tell me how she longed for his return to her but worried she'd grown haggard while he was gone, so many troubles and lonely thoughts had she carried in her heart. He did not see her that way.

Glory Lake Luncheon
Chicken Salad

2 cups cooked chicken, chopped or pulled into bite sized pieces

1 celery stalk, chopped

1 green onion, chopped

1 handful of grapes, halved

2 tablespoons mayonnaise, or more, to taste

1 teaspoon Dijon Mustard

Pinch of salt

Pinch of tarragon

When Pop and Martin returned to my lakeside feeling-sorry-for-myself-blanket, we munched our delicious lunch, which was accompanied by a history lesson from the ever-talkative Pop.

"Did you know that the **Chocolate Chip Cookie** was invented by accident?" Pop began. "In 1933, Ruth Wakefield was making her famous **Chocolate Butter Drop Do Cookies** for her guests at her Toll House Inn, but didn't have any baker's chocolate. She chopped up and substituted a semi-sweet chocolate bar that had been a gift from her friend, Andrew Nestle. To her chagrin, the chocolate did not melt, but just softened into the dough. Hence, the Toll House **Chocolate Chip Cookie** was born!

"The enterprising Mr. Nestle began including Mrs. Wakefield's recipe and a small chopping tool with his Semi-sweet Chocolate Bar, then got even smarter, and by 1939, he'd invented chocolate chips. Nestle's was built into a $130 million dollar company - and that lucky lady, Mrs. Wakefield, received a lifetime supply of chocolate chips."

Pop threw a crumb to Major, who loved a good cookie.

Years later, I found the signature "Ruth Wakefield" in the Big House Guest Book. Could it have been?

An Interesting Puzzle to Solve

If you analyze the Chocolate Drop Do recipe below, the chocolate is melted into the butter before being blended with the sugar. I have a little hunch the non-melting chocolate legend has been stretched. Unfortunately, Ruth Wakefield died in 1977 and the Toll house Inn in Whitman, Massachusetts, burned down in 1984. Alas, no one to ask.

Chocolate Chip Cookies

2 1/4 cups all-purpose flour

1 teaspoon baking soda

1 teaspoon salt

1 cup (2 sticks) butter, softened

1/4 cup granulated sugar

1 cup packed brown sugar

1 teaspoon vanilla extract

2 large eggs

2 cups (12-oz. pkg.) Semi-Sweet Chocolate Morsels

1 cup chopped nuts (optional)

Preheat oven to 375°

Combine flour, baking soda and salt in small bowl. Beat butter, granulated sugar, brown sugar and vanilla extract in large mixer bowl until creamy. Add eggs, one at a time, beating well after each addition. Gradually beat in flour mixture. Stir in chocolate chips and nuts. Drop by rounded tablespoon onto parchment lined baking sheets. Makes 5 dozen cookies.

Bake for 9 to 11 minutes or until golden brown. Cool on baking sheets for 2 minutes; remove to wire racks to cool completely.

Pan Cookie: Grease 15 x 10-inch jelly-roll pan. Prepare dough as above. Spread into prepared pan. Bake for 20 to 25 minutes or until golden brown. Cool in pan on wire rack. Makes 4 dozen bars.

Slice and Bake Cookie: Prepare dough as above. Divide in half; wrap in waxed paper. Refrigerate for 1 hour or until firm. Shape each half into 15-inch log; wrap in wax paper. Refrigerate for 30 minutes. Preheat oven to 375°. Cut into 1/2-inch-thick slices; place on ungreased baking sheets. Bake for 8 to 10 minutes or until golden brown. Cool on baking sheets for 2 minutes; remove to wire racks to cool completely.

Chocolate Butter Drop Do Cookies

1/2 cup butter
1/4 cup (2oz) baker's chocolate
2 cups all-purpose flour
1 teaspoon baking powder
1/4 teaspoon salt
1 cup packed brown sugar
1/2 cup granulated sugar
1 large egg
1/2 cup milk
1 cup finely chopped pecans

Preheat oven to 350°. Combine flour, baking powder and salt in a bowl. In a separate ceramic bowl, combine chocolate and butter. Melt the chocolate and butter in the top of a double boiler.

Add sugars and egg to the chocolate. Add half of your dry ingredients to chocolate mixture and stir until completely combined. Stir in milk and dry ingredients. Fold in chopped pecans with a spoon.

Place a piece of parchment on a baking sheet. Drop small amounts of dough onto cookie sheet by rounded teaspoonful.

Bake for approximately 10 minutes. Makes about 5 dozen cookies.

To bake as bar cookies, spread the dough in a sprayed pan until approximately 1/4 to 1/2 inch thick. Bake about 20 minutes or until done. Cut into bars when cool.

Store cookies in an airtight container.

Homecoming

Major was sprawled on the front porch of the Big House, enjoying the shade on a warm and humid Sunday morning. The Farm was quiet, the staff languid and the Farm animals still as stone. Major's elegant ears pricked at the faint sound of a car from far down the mile-long driveway. He sat up straight and let out a low whimper.

"Daddy's home! He's here! Daddy's home!"

We knew that Major knew.

And there, of a sudden, he was, in his khaki uniform, getting out of a cab. He was handsome and spare — a near stranger kept vivid in our minds by Gloria: she listened to his music, read his stories, played the Little Red Hen over and over again when we asked. James had left us at the Farm and traveled thousands of lonely miles across the water, helping to make way for the marching boots of democracy. And his own boots, covering the toes of a musician in an indoor, fairly civilized administrative job, had, even so, left their tread upon many miles of foreign dirt.

Gloria sat James down at the oak table and made him fresh coffee. They chattered and laughed and hugged and cried and laughed and hugged some more. She cut him a slice of **German Chocolate Cake,** hands fumbling with the knife. He put me on his knee - I was mildly squiggly and nervous myself. Martin hung back, shyness and longing written in tandem on his face. Soon, Martin, too, was in the arms of his Daddy, *and* Gloria, and we were all together again, quietly embraced in an eight-armed huddle of Love. We made no sound.

German Chocolate Cake

Preheat oven to 350°
3 9 inch cake pans,
buttered and floured
Baking Spray
1 4 oz. Package Sweet German Chocolate
1/2 cup boiling water
1 cup butter
2 cups sugar
4 egg yolks

1 teaspoon vanilla
2 1/2 cups cake flour
1 teaspoon baking soda
1/2 teaspoon salt
1 cup buttermilk
4 stiffly beaten egg whites

Melt chocolate in boiling water. Cream the butter and sugar until light. (This can be done with your hands — makes a great blend!) Add egg yolks one at a time, blending well each time. Add vanilla and melted chocolate and mix well. Sift flour with soda and salt. To the chocolate mixture, add sifted dry ingredients alternately with buttermilk. Don't beat hard — just mix well. Fold in beaten egg whites. Spread batter evenly between three buttered and floured cake pans. Bake at 350° for 35-40 minutes. Cool.

Frosting

1 cup half and half
1 cup Bakers' Fine sugar
3 egg yolks
1/4 pound softened butter
1 teaspoon vanilla

Place all ingredients in a saucepan and cook over medium heat for about fifteen minutes, stirring constantly, until thickened. Add one cup coconut and one cup chopped pecans. Beat with wooden spoon until of spreading consistency. Let cool a few minutes. Spread between layers and on top (not the sides) of cake.

Pot Roast
In James' Top Ten

1 Tbsp. flour
1 tsp. salt
1/8 tsp. pepper
1/2 tsp. dried thyme leaves
1-1/2 lb. boneless beef top round, cut into 6 pieces
1 Tbsp. olive oil
4 potatoes, peeled, cut into chunks
2 cups carrots, cut in chunks
3 stalks celery
1 onion, chopped
2 cloves garlic
2 cups stock
1 tsp. Worcestershire sauce
2 Tbsp. cornstarch
1/4 cup cooled stock

Combine flour, salt, pepper, and thyme in a plastic bag and toss beef with this mixture. Cook beef pieces in olive oil in a crockpot for 2-3 minutes on each side to brown.

Pour beef stock and Worcestershire sauce over meat. Cover crockpot and cook on low for 8-10 hours until beef is tender.

Combine potatoes, carrots and onion the crockpot with beef. Cook until vegetables are tender but not overcooked, 30 minutes to an hour.

Remove meat and vegetables from crockpot and place on serving platter. Cover with foil to keep warm and place in low oven. Combine cornstarch and cooled stock in a small bowl and mix well with fork or whisk. Add to liquid in crockpot, turn to high and cook for 10-15 minutes until gravy is thickened. Serve with beef and vegetables. 6 servings

Chicken Stew with Dumplings
In James' Top Ten

Stew:
3 tablespoons cooking oil
1 large onion, diced
2 cloves garlic
2 carrots, diced
1 stalk celery, diced
1 chicken, roasted and shredded
6 cups chicken stock
1 tablespoon fresh chopped Italian parsley
2 bay leaves
Salt and pepper

Dumplings:
1 cup milk
1/2 cup butter

1/2 teaspoon salt
1/2 teaspoon nutmeg
1 cup purpose flour
3 eggs

In cooking oil, sauté the onion, carrots and celery. Add stock, celery salt, parsley and bay leaves. Simmer until the barley is tender, about 30 minutes. Add shredded roasted chicken.

Make dumplings:

Bring the milk and butter to simmer, add salt and nutmeg. Remove from heat and immediately add flour stirring until dough leaves the sides of the pan. Blend in the eggs, 1 at a time, forming a sticky dough.

Season the soup, to taste, with salt and pepper. Add small spoonsful of dumpling dough and simmer until dumplings rise. Remove dumplings from pot, place aside. Serve stew and place a dumpling on top of each serving.

"Aroma vs. Odor"

The aromas in the Big House kitchen created a perfumery of nourishment. Identifying fragrances was a hobby worth cultivating in a place like that.

T and I sat at the plank table, drawing paper dolls and wardrobes of paper clothes, coloring, watching and ever alert to the homely sounds of Flossie and Bessie's voices. Gazing out the big window I pondered Lincoln in some kind of garden dance with Hank, Buster and Polly, the exotic scarecrows in our grandparent's cast-off clothes. Marnie's old purple silk dress draped uncomfortably over Polly's straw stuffed body, but Hank and Buster carried Pop's pants and shirts with a bit more dignity. Lincoln whistled Brahms Lullaby and Beethoven's 5th to the beans and squash while pulling weeds. His love songs lightly tapped on our hearts through the window, "I sing to make them beans grrrow for me, Honey," he'd drawl.

The kitchen emanated warmth, with dense, humid wafts of bubbling jam and whiffs of rising yeasted rolls. There was usually a pie or cake. It was Heaven, pure and simple.

And then it happened — the first smell ever to rock me out of my little haven of sustenance.

James had been home about a few weeks. Gloria was still going through her list of James' Top Ten - happifying dinners.

It wasn't a smell. It was an odor. It stunk!

274

Liver and Onions! Gloria tried to disguise it with bacon. She opened all the windows. She told me it was good for me. She told me the smell and the flavor would grow on me.

Gloria was sadly mistaken, but she didn't give it up. No. That evening she sat Little Glory down at the formal dining room table, candelabra, damask cloth, good silver and all. It was a full family affair — Mother, the Homecoming Man, Martin, Pop and Marnie, Aunt Tournier and Big Jon, my cousins Little Jon and T, Jr. Glumly I sat looking at everything but my plate. The little calf's organ sat quivering in front of me, smothered under all those layers of necessary diversions. The lovely smell of bacon was temporarily spoiled. I was not impressed. I was five. Give me a break! Liver and Onions!

Sit there I did, though, even after all others had left the table and gone on to their hobbies and homework. As she squiggled and scrammed out of the room, I gave T the evil eye, feeling betrayed by her seeming enjoyment (not to mention completion!) of such a disagreeable dinner. Later, I discovered that she had secretly fed her little piece of animal organ to Major, who was under the table, quietly snarfing it up like any right-minded, Army-trained German Shepherd. Liver was OK for him. Just not for me.

And still I sat. Martin was gone. Father was tapping piano keys in the other room — I could hear my favorite, "Clair de Lune." Major was gone by then, too, having followed his new BFF, who still had the smell of the luscious liver clinging to her little fingertips, out the door. Gloria was in and out of the dining room, determined to keep me at the table until I had at least tried the dreaded stuff. I almost made it. I placed a bit on the tip of my fork and brought it close to my lips. The fork clattered to the plate and then fell on the floor. There was no way.

I squirmed and fidgeted. I pinched and played with the golden, two-tone tablecloth. I imagined dramatic endings to this story to tell my friends. I murmured five-year-old invectives against determined mothers, stupid cows, betraying cousins, abandoning brothers.

Finally, at 10 o'clock, James came to my rescue. He was the only one who could, of course, being in the rarified space of the husband returned to his lover. He could do no wrong. He lobbied with Gloria on my behalf, sighting all the other foods I enjoyed, all the love I bore for the care and feeding of the family, and certainly all the other ways I might get enough iron.

When I was finally freed of my imaginary dining-room-prison shackles, my butt was sore from three hours of sitting on the hard, straight-backed chairs and my little heart was broken to feel such punishment engendered for such a thing as Liver and Onions. James tenderly escorted me to our cottage, having witnessed the glare I sent in Gloria's general direction. As he put me to bed, he whispered a promise.

"No more Liver and Onions, ever," he said. "What shall we make tomorrow?"

"Milk Chocolate Cake," I whispered, nodding off.

Milk Chocolate Cake

1/2 cup butter
1 1/2 cups sugar
2 eggs
1 cup sour milk
2 cups sifted cake flour
2 squares or 2 oz. milk chocolate
1/2 teaspoon salt
1 teaspoon vanilla
1 teaspoon vinegar
1 teaspoon soda

Melt the chocolate. Set aside. Cream the butter. Gradually add the sugar. Add one egg. Beat. Add the other egg. Beat two minutes. Add the vanilla then add the flour and milk, alternately. Add melted chocolate. Last, add soda dissolved in vinegar.

Preheat oven to 350°. Pour into 2 prepared 9 inch layers or 3 8 inch layers. Bake at 350° for about 25 minutes.

Fill and frost with whipped cream and/or drizzle with **Chocolate Sauce**.

Chocolate Sauce

6 oz chocolate (dark or milk)

4 oz water

1 oz butter

6 tbsp cream

3 tbsp sugar

1/2 tsp vanilla

In a medium sized saucepan heat the water and sugar, stirring constantly to dissolve the sugar. Bring to a boil, stirring until all of the sugar has been dissolved.Break the chocolate into small pieces and cut the butter into small chunks. Add to the pan of water and sugar and stir. Remove the pan from the heat and stir the sauce until the chocolate and butter have melted and all the ingredients have blended together. Stir in the cream and the vanilla.

Serve the chocolate sauce immediately while warm.

When James returned, he most often made breakfast, sometimes in the cottage, perhaps on Sundays at the Big House. He would wrap himself in an ample apron and rather *conduct* the morning. He brought the record player into the cottage kitchen and played music while we ate — John Phillips Souza marches to wake us up, then Bach, Beethoven & Brahms.

He let Martin and me have whatever we wanted for breakfast, provided it was hot. Bacon Sandwiches with Durkee's Famous Sauce was a favorite. So were Hot Dogs, Campbell's Beef & Barley Soup, Burgers and Warm Apple Pie with a piece of cheddar cheese melted on top.

And, of course, we remembered his **World's Greatest Pancakes**, lighter than feathers.

In James' own words:
The World's Greatest Pancakes

3 eggs
2 cups flour (all purpose, sifted)
2 1/2 cups buttermilk
1/2 teaspoon salt

1 heaping teaspoon baking powder
1 teaspoon baking soda
1 tablespoon melted butter
1 tablespoon warm syrup

About an hour ahead of time, separate the whites of the eggs from the yolk. Let whites come to room temperature. Return yolks to ice box.

Preheat griddle to 400° (don't grease griddle).

When ready to proceed, put buttermilk in mixing bowl and add the soda. Stir. Put flour in another bowl and add the salt and baking powder. Beat yolks and stir thoroughly into the buttermilk mixture. Stir in the dry ingredients. Stir thoroughly — don't beat. Add butter and syrup. Stir, don't beat.

When griddle is ready, beat egg whites until they form soft peaks, then fold whites into rest of mixture. Using a cooking spoon, drop spoonsful of the batter onto the dry griddle, spreading lightly until each pancake is a little larger than a silver dollar (*the old kind*, he wrote). Bake until air holes pop open and remain open. Turn once. Serve golden brown. Makes approximately 40 two-inch pancakes.

Note: Serve on warm plates with warm syrup and butter. Doesn't make sense to have hot cakes but cold plates, butter and syrup. For a special taste treat, try strawberries and sour cream instead of syrup. (These, of course, should be cold).

If these pancakes don't practically float off the griddle, you did something wrong.

James developed a sweet habit of getting in Gloria's way in the kitchen, especially during Happy Hour, a custom he brought home from the Sea. He liked his Martinis with just a whisper of vermouth and an olive or onion. No twist for him. James took Gloria in his arms and waltzed her around the kitchen, laughing. He sang her the love songs he'd tapped out on his knee onboard the cargo ship to Japan.

"I love what I see when I look in your eyes, my Gloria…"
"Hey, you! I'm making dinner here." She's laughing.
"The love that is there like the sun lights the skies, my Gloria…"
"The rolls are burning."
"The one hope for me is that I'll always see, my Gloria…"
She reaches out to turn off the timer and turns back to face her man.
"I'm lucky, I know, I can claim you for mine, my Gloria…"
He kisses her ear.
"I promise to love you as long as stars shine, my Glo…ri…. aaaaaaaa…"

Fourth of July

While we packed our baskets for a Glory Lake picnic (cold chicken, **Deviled Eggs**, **Potato Salad**, the ubiquitous **Ambrosia, Date Bread**), James was listening to the radio, wondering what President Truman was doing at a baseball game, when he was supposed to be on his knees, having declared July 4th, 1952 a National Day of Prayer.

"Well then," he said, rising from his chair and looking at his little family, as if he'd quite made up his mind, "perhaps we should stay home and pray, ourselves!"

What? No picnic? Three pairs of eyes stared back at James in horror.

"Just kidding," he said, with a twinkle in his eye.

"Let's go and appreciate this Glorious day together, in our own way."

On the way to Glory Lake, James, Gloria, Martin and Little Glory sang this song together:

The Teddy Bears' Picnic

If you go out in the woods today

You're sure of a big surprise.

If you go out in the woods today

You'd better go in disguise.

For every bear that ever there was

Will gather there for certain, because

Today's the day the teddy bears have their picnic.

If you go out in the woods today,

You'd better not go alone.

It's lovely out in the woods today,

But safer to stay at home.

For every bear that ever there was

Will gather there for certain, because

Today's the day the teddy bears have their picnic

Every teddy bear, that's been good

Is sure of a treat today

There's lots of wonderful things to eat

And wonderful games to play

Beneath the trees, where nobody sees

They'll hide and seek as long as they please

Today's the day the teddy bears have their picnic

Deviled Eggs
6 eggs
1/4 cup fresh Aioli
1 teaspoon white vinegar
1 teaspoon Dijon mustard
Pinch tarragon
1/8 teaspoon salt
black pepper
paprika, for garnish

Place eggs in a single layer in a saucepan and cover with water. Bring to boil, turn the heat down, and simmer for 5 minutes. Remove from heat and let stand for 10 minutes. Rinse under cold water continuously for 1 minute.

Cool and carefully peel eggs. Slice the eggs in half lengthwise, placing yolks in a bowl, and the whites on a platter. Mash the yolks and mix with Aioli, vinegar, mustard, tarragon, salt, and pepper.

Mound teaspoons of the yolk mixture into the egg whites. Sprinkle with paprika and serve.

James
Fourth of July, 1952
Thoughts

When mortal man at last decides
To stop his wars — and peace abides
And mothers stop their tears for sons
And all may stay with loved ones
Why, then I think there will be strife
O'er who can live the better life!

Wars will stop and fighting cease
When a man with himself becomes at peace
His knowledge good, his motives pure
His thoughts of life at last secure
When each shall cease to envy all
Why, then I think he can't be small.

Shall we as humans hope to see
The day when this shall come to be?
I fear not so, for such a thing
Takes love and strength of which we sing
But sing we only — never act
And thus we miss the point exact.

Love one another, is part, yes
But more important, love self less!

Farm-style Potato Salad

8 med red potatoes, cooked and diced
1 1/2 cups mayonnaise
2 tablespoons cider vinegar
2 tablespoons sugar
1 tablespoon yellow mustard
1 teaspoon salt
1 garlic clove, crushed
1/2 teaspoon pepper
2 celery ribs, sliced
1/2 cup finely chopped onion
4 hard-boiled eggs, chopped
paprika
Large Leaf lettuce

Place diced cooked potatoes in a large bowl.

Mix mayonnaise, vinegar, sugar, mustard, salt, garlic and pepper in another bowl. Add this mixture to the potatoes. Add celery and onions, mix well. Stir in chopped eggs. Serve on a bed of lettuce.

Date Bread

300°
One loaf pan or two small loaf pans
Baking spray
2 eggs
2 cups dark brown sugar
2/3 cup canola oil
1 tablespoon vanilla

2 cupsflour
1 tablespoon baking powder
1/2 teaspoon salt
1 cup buttermilk
1 cup chopped date pieces

Preheat oven to 300°. Blend first four ingredients in Kitchenaid or other mixer. Combine flour, baking soda and salt and add to egg mixture, alternating with buttermilk. Pour into loaf pan. Add date pieces and stir. Bake about 30 minutes. Remove from pans to cool. Delicious with cream cheese.

James
July 5ᵗʰ, 1952
Note left for Gloria
by the coffeepot in the Cottage:

Good Morning, Glorious Gloria,
Made your coffee.
Restless as a cat in a crowd
Took a piece of your
Date Bread with
some cheese.
Walking the fields.

I am home.

The End

Alphabetical Recipe Index

Photos

The Farm in Snow
Glory in San Francisco
Gloria
Musical notes for "Gloria"
Martin & Glory at the Farm
Major
Mr. Talbot
Cousins
Lincoln
Hay Harvest
Harmon
Garden Plot
James

Acknowledgments

I give thanks to my family, living and late, but particularly to:

My grandfather, for the Farm, the canvas on which this story is painted;

The real Flossie, Bessie and Lincoln, for generosity of spirit;

My mother, for love;

My father, whose poetry and songs reach out to touch me from shadows;

My brothers;

My son;

Joan Marsh, whose love for and belief in me speaks volumes, and whose opinion I would value, even if she weren't an editor with skills;

Sandra McCauley for seeing four books, not one, and who set me free to explore the Farm in all its, uhm... Glory;

Erin Palmer, for deep friendship, many readings and honest opinions;

Melissa Lofton, for daily creative inspiration;

and David Gordon, for enthusiastically enjoying all my 20th century tests and historic recipes; for 21st Century web-design; and for all-around general love, kindness and fellow-inquisitiveness.

Ginna BB Gordon
Carmel, 2011

Author's Afterword

As James and Gloria explore each other's personal real estate, the Farm Folk settle back down, like pigeons on a sidewalk after a fluttering, cacophonic disturbance. Pop and Marnie fly away for a long journey abroad. Gloria, after months of loneliness, sees again her reflection in her lover's eyes and **Honey Baby Darlin'** continues:

Book Two - Face the Music
Glory matures into young womanhood, stirs a dash of trouble into the simmering soup of her life and sets off for Carmel, California, where she plants a garden, rears her child and considers the thoughts and nutritional habits of a few select spiritual teachers and good cooks. It is the 60s, and her pantry bulges with whole grains, the window sills carry trays of sprouting seeds, and chickens once again scratch 'n scrabble in the backyard.

Book Three - To the Stars
Glory cooks for gurus, spas, rock stars, and other illustrious beings while managing her own personal affairs. She lives in a 400 square foot tipi at a retreat farm and discovers an enlightening genealogical fact. As she travels the west coast in her red Jeep Cherokee, Glory creates kitchen temples of nourishment while serving up sustenance in warm bowls. She writes a cookbook about Ayurveda and becomes a grandmother.

Book Four - My Carmel

Glory, longing for a home and a hearth of her own, settles back to Carmel, opens Morning, Glory Café and, eventually, finally, finds herself in the arms of her Beloved. Then she writes another book. And then another.

GINNA BB GORDON
Author Bio

Ginna has cooked for movie stars, Tibetan Lamas, gurus, and teachers; for retreat and conference centers; and for her own catering companies and cafes, in very unusual situations (cook tents, tall ships, mountain lodges, trailers on a movie set, spa kitchens, campfires).

Ginna was founding executive chef at Deepak Chopra's Center for Well Being in La Jolla, California, where she designed the original kitchen, created the spa meals and operated a 24-seat café at the Center.

She and David Simon, MD, the Chopra Center medical director, co-authored *A Simple Celebration: a vegetarian cookbook for body mind and spirit,* (Ginna Bell Bragg, Harmony Books/Random House, 1997, ISBN0-517-70732-2). This book is for the vegetarian home cook interested in the practice of Ayurveda, the lifestyle based on ancient East Indian rishi-knowledge. Using Western ingredients, Ginna offers meals and reference guide for ingredients and body types.

Ginna's new book, *Honey, Baby, Darlin', Book One The Farm,* is the first part of *a serial memoir about cooking, love and the love of cooking.*

Ginna lives with her husband, singer/ web-guru, David Gordon, and their cat, Squeaks, in Carmel, California. Her father served in Korea from September, 1951 to June, 1952. Her grandfather, Jess Grover Bell, founded Bonne Bell Cosmetics in 1927. And her mother, Virginia, was his oldest daughter.

Would you like to see your manuscript become a book?

If you are interested in becoming a PublishAmerica author, please submit your manuscript for possible publication to us at:

acquisitions@publishamerica.com

You may also mail in your manuscript to:

**PublishAmerica
PO Box 151
Frederick, MD 21705**

www.publishamerica.com

PUBLISHAMERICA

CPSIA information can be obtained at www.ICGtesting.com
Printed in the USA
LVOW120823190112

264504LV00002B/28/P